T5-BYJ-988

# Praise for *Authentic Intellectual Work*

"Newmann and colleagues offer a refreshing approach to research and professional development, which deeply honors teachers' critical inquiry and collaboration. Thanks to their insights, educators finally have a framework for promoting rigor and relevance across all grades and subjects. Those who join this journey will reap the rewards of increased teacher engagement and improved student learning."

**Linda Darling-Hammond**
*Charles E. Ducommun Professor of Education, Stanford University*

"*Authentic Intellectual Work* provides an effective framework for educators as we move from unpacking CCSS to a focus on instruction and assessment. Your entire community will appreciate this research and evidenced based approach to closing significant achievement gaps through a focus on what matters most—engaging our youth in meaningful work that prepares them for college and careers. Add this to your must-read list!"

**Jill Gildea**
*Superintendent of Schools, Fremont School
District 79, Mundelein, IL*

"In a time when education and the world focus too much on testing, Newmann, Carmichael, and King present a set a compelling alternatives based on in-depth research and experience. Their emphasis on rigor will support meaningful learning and transcend some of the silliness we all confront daily."

**Peter Dillon**
*Superintendent of Schools, Berkshire
Hills Regional School District, Stockbridge, MA*

"Schools are looking for ways to help staff transition to the Common Core and that involves significant changes in the type of work teachers use with students. *Authentic Intellectual Work* appears to be a great way to make that happen."

**Richard A. Simon**
*Adjunct Instructor Educational Administration,
Stony Brook University and LIU Post, Roslyn, NY*

"*Authentic Intellectual Work* is a powerful design for enhancing success for students across ability, ethnicity, and socioeconomics. Although similar ideas have been introduced in the field of education, AIW provides clear parameters for instruction that is authentic."

**Debbie Tracht**
*Learning Specialist, Professional Development Provider,
Addison Northwest Supervisory Union, Vergennes, VT*

"AIW serves as the foundation for systemic change by providing tools that allows teachers to take risks and be reflective of their practices in the ever changing landscape of education."

**Lesley Stancarone**
*Principal, New Haven, CT*

"Many school administrators, teachers, and parents have responded to the adoption of the Common Core State Standards with a mixture of fear, loathing, and panic. Newmann, Carmichael, and King explain how the AIW framework can enable educators to overcome those fears while building the culture of collaboration and trust required for successful school reform. Importantly, they also show how collective professional development · among teachers and school leaders can enhance educators' learning and practice leading to improved, more equitable student outcomes."

*Greg Anrig*
*Vice President of The Century Foundation and Author of*
Beyond the Education Wars: Evidence That Collaboration Builds Effective Schools

"Since my first encounter with AIW, I've been inspired because it isn't about formulas or panaceas. Rather, this framework is about the meaningful unpacking of practice in a way that connects us to our classrooms and helps us see rigor as a catalyst, not an imposition. In short, it's a cornerstone of my practice."

*Sarah Brown Wessling*
*2010 National Teacher of*
*the Year, Teacher Laureate Teaching Channel*

"*Authentic Intellectual Work: Improving Teaching for Rigorous Learning* offers educators a valuable framework for constructing the kinds of learning we would hope all of our students experience—grounded in serious inquiry around the topics well—equipped citizens must be prepared to address in an informed society. Just as important, the authors assist school and system leaders in building educator capacity to create these learning experiences in schools, recognizing that schools cannot achieve the aims of any rigorous student standards without first ensuring that educators are well supported and prepared to teach in differing and demanding ways."

*Stephanie Hirsh*
*Executive Director Learning Forward*

"This important new book is a tremendous resource for teachers, school administrators, and policymakers. Rooted in more than 20 years of rigorous research, this exceptionally clear and example-packed book makes a compelling case for why Authentic Intellectual Work should be at the centerpiece of the school curriculum— across all grades and subjects."

*Diana Hess*
*Dean of the School of Education and Professor in the*
*Department of Curriculum and Instruction University of Wisconsin-Madison*

"This is the definitive volume on Authentic Intellectual Work. It will guide educators in the collaboration they need to challenge each other's practices toward ever-increasing rigor, a fundamental building block of 21st century learning."

*Ken Kay*
*CEO EdLeader21*

"*Authentic Intellectual Work* has had a profound impact on policy, practice, and research in Australia for nearly two decades. Both the research and the professional development presented in this volume are compelling."

*Jennifer Gore*
*Professor and Director Teachers and Teaching*
*Research Program, University of Newcastle, Australia*

# Authentic Intellectual Work

*Improving Teaching for Rigorous Learning*

Fred M. Newmann

Dana L. Carmichael

M. Bruce King

CORWIN
A SAGE Company

FOR INFORMATION:

Corwin
A SAGE Company
2455 Teller Road
Thousand Oaks, California 91320
(800) 233-9936
www.corwin.com

SAGE Publications Ltd.
1 Oliver's Yard
55 City Road
London EC1Y 1SP
United Kingdom

SAGE Publications India Pvt. Ltd.
B 1/I 1 Mohan Cooperative Industrial Area
Mathura Road, New Delhi 110 044
India

SAGE Publications Asia-Pacific Pte. Ltd.
3 Church Street
#10-04 Samsung Hub
Singapore 049483

Acquisitions Editor:  Dan Alpert
Associate Editor:  Kimberly Greenberg
Editorial Assistant:  Katie Crilley
Production Editor:  Amy Schroller
Copy Editor:  Sarah J. Duffy
Typesetter:  C&M Digitals (P) Ltd.
Proofreader:  Ellen Brink
Indexer:  Judy Hunt
Cover Designer:  Scott Van Atta
Marketing Manager:  Kimberly Kanake

Copyright © 2016 by Corwin

Printed in the United States of America

*Library of Congress Cataloging-in-Publication Data*

Names: Newmann, Fred M., author. | Carmichael, Dana, author. | King, M. Bruce, author.

Title: Authentic intellectual work : improving teaching for rigorous learning / Fred M. Newmann, Dana Carmichael, M. Bruce King.

Description: Thousand Oaks, Calif.: Corwin, 2016. | Includes bibliographical references and index.

Identifiers: LCCN 2015029406 | ISBN 9781483381084 (pbk. : alk. paper)

Subjects: LCSH: Teachers--Professional relationships—United States. | Effective teaching—United States. | Academic achievement—United States.

Classification: LCC LB1775.2 .N49 2016 | DDC 371.102—dc23 LC record available at http://lccn.loc.gov/2015029406

This book is printed on acid-free paper.

15 16 17 18 19 10 9 8 7 6 5 4 3 2 1

# Contents

# Acknowledgments

In 2007 Rita Martens at the Iowa Department of Education, with support from Jim Reese and the leadership of then-Director Judy Jefferies, invited us to begin a professional development project to help teachers apply the conceptual framework for Authentic Intellectual Work developed at the University of Wisconsin in the 1990s. Rita's understanding of the research, how to conduct professional development that teachers value, and her amazing energy and skills in working with department staff and practitioners throughout the state, along with Jim's foresight and ability to secure adequate funding, launched and sustained the project long enough for us now to summarize how teachers, administrators, and professional development specialists far beyond Iowa can benefit from the project.

This book draws on contributions from dozens of researchers and hundreds of administrators and teachers over three decades. We regret that we cannot name and thank all who have influenced this work, but we are immeasurably grateful for their participation, critical inquiry, and material support in developing the framework for Authentic Intellectual Work (AIW) and in shaping an approach to professional development that enriches instruction.

Professional development leaders and coaches, working in diverse schools, districts, and other organizations, made countless contributions to improve teaching and learning through AIW: Katy Evenson, Teresa Bellinghausen, Tina Wahlert, Susie Peterson, Warren Weber, Elli Wiemers, Pat Briese, Jen Savery, Gretchen Kriegel, Tammie McKenzie, Kevin Hosband, Lucinda Boyd, Dan Breyfogle, Laura Kautman, Jodi Hurn, Joe Mueting, Meg Frideres, Mark Solomon, Melissa Hesner, Janelle Schorg, Maryann Angeroth, Deborah Humpal Cleveland, Becca Lindahl, Fred Nolan, Jen Savery, Paul Spies, Kathy Lemberger, and Mary Schmidt.

Thanks to teachers and their students for sharing examples of tasks, lessons, and student work included and discussed in Part II: Lucinda Boyd, Amy Doll, Robyn Ponder, April Gilbert, Mike Thompson, Tammy O'Connor, Kent Muyskens, Shannon Johnson, Benjamin Deal, Jody Stone, Lindsay Ryan, and Angela Wink.

Allison Berryhill, Laura Hensley, Emily Kobliska, Tim Lutz, and Pennie Rude gave permission to publish, as "perspectives from the field," excerpts from their reflections on coaching.

Jennifer Cadell, Jenney Stevens, and Erica Wallace provided excellent technical support in preparing the publication. Dan Alpert, Kimberley Greenburg, and Cesar Reyes of Corwin offered superb assistance in publishing it.

Warmest thanks to our families for their encouragement and support, not only in preparing the book but also during the years of prior work that made it possible.

## About the Authors

**Dr. Fred M. Newmann,** Emeritus Professor of Curriculum and Instruction, University of Wisconsin–Madison, began his education career teaching high school history and social studies in 1959. Dissatisfied with prevailing curriculum and instruction, he completed doctoral studies at Harvard University and began to attack the broader question: In what ways can institutions, especially schools, in a modern culture be shaped to enhance community?

This led to research and development of social studies and civic education curriculum; planning an alternative school; studies of alienation in secondary schools; theories of democratic citizenship; student community service; higher order thinking in high school curriculum; new approaches to student assessment; the restructuring of public; elementary, middle, and high schools; and professional development to build capacity in low-income schools.

At Wisconsin, he taught graduate courses in curriculum and assessment and directed national centers on effective secondary schools and on organization and restructuring of schools (K–12), which generated the initial research on Authentic Intellectual Work that was used in research on Chicago Public School reform. He has published widely and is recognized internationally as a leader in reform of curriculum, instruction, and schooling. He retired from the University of Wisconsin in 2001, and since 2007 he has helped develop the approach to professional development sponsored by the Center for Authentic Intellectual Work.

**Dr. Dana L. Carmichael** began her teaching career in Japan in 1987. After 5 years, she joined Minneapolis Public Schools as a social studies teacher. In 1995, Dana earned a Fulbright-Hayes Teacher Exchange Scholarship to write authentic curriculum in Namibia on how education promotes democracy in new nations. Her international background, which included living in Chile, Spain, and Austria as a child, led her to pursue a PhD in comparative international development in education studies in the Department of Policy and Administration at the University of Minnesota–Twin Cities, which she completed in 2003.

Ultimately her passion for teaching urban students kept her in the Twin Cities. She first learned about Dr. Newmann's work in the mid-1990s while serving as the K–12 district social studies curriculum specialist. She and Dr. Patricia Avery (University of Minnesota) collaborated on a number of early Authentic Intellectual Work (AIW) projects. Her experiences directing these projects, including a Minnesota Best Practices grant (2000) and a federal Teaching American History Grant (2001–2004), combined with additional experiences, including as director of NCLB for Minneapolis Public Schools, staff development director for Bloomington Public Schools, and Learning Forward academy graduate (2007), prepared her to accept Newmann's invitation to join him and Dr. King on the Iowa-AIW project. Since 2008, she has served as executive director of the Center for Authentic Intellectual Work, based in Saint Paul, Minnesota, where she lives with her husband and two children. For more information about how the Center supports educators in learning to sustain transformational reform by promoting academic rigor through collaborative inquiry and reflection, visit www.centerforaiw.com.

**Dr. M. Bruce King** is a faculty associate with the Department of Educational Leadership and Policy Analysis (ELPA) at the University of Wisconsin–Madison. His work in ELPA concentrates on teaching courses on instructional leadership and teacher capacity, coordinating the Wisconsin Idea PhD cohort program in K–12 leadership and building effective partnerships between the department and schools and districts.

Bruce has been a researcher with the Wisconsin Center for Education Research, where he contributed to two studies focused on Authentic Intellectual Work, the Research Institute on Secondary Education Reform for Youth with Disabilities, and the Center for Organization and Restructuring of Schools. He received his PhD in curriculum and instruction from UW–Madison and taught upper elementary, middle, and high school for 11 years in Wisconsin; Minnesota; and Quito, Ecuador.

Bruce was recently a research fellow at the University of Newcastle, New South Wales, and has consulted on two research projects in Australian schools that extended the body of research on AIW. He has published in national and international research and practitioner journals. Currently, he is an AIW lead coach in Iowa, Wisconsin, and Georgia, and he contributes to professional development sponsored by the Center for Authentic Intellectual Work.

# Introduction

**PURPOSE**

Since the 1980s, U.S. student achievement data often show low student competence in academic subjects, problem-solving skills, communication, and use of technology and other specialized occupational skills. Importantly, major disparities in achievement exist among student groups by race and ethnicity and by economic and disability status. Intense competition with other nations for highly skilled labor has dramatized shortcomings in U.S. education. Recently, a movement to improve U.S. education through the Common Core State Standards has aimed to address these shortcomings by specifying more rigorous intellectual work. The Common Core State Standards emphasize curriculum content: the subjects, topics within subjects, specific material, and general skills that all students should master at different grade levels. Many states and districts have adopted the standards, and some vary in the specific language used. Some typical standards are listed below.

---

**Examples of Common Core State Standards
and Next Generation Science Standards**

Grade 1 Reading/Literature: Explain major differences between books that tell stories and books that give information, drawing on a wide reading of a range of text types.

Grade 3 Mathematics: Determine the unknown whole number in a multiplication or division equation relating three whole numbers. For example, determine the unknown number that makes the equation true in each of the equations $8 \times ? = 48$, $5 = \_ \div 3$, $6 \times 6 = ?$

Grades 6–8 History/Social Studies: Identify key steps in a text's description of a process related to history/social studies (e.g., how a bill becomes law, how interest rates are raised or lowered).

Grades 6–8 Science: Develop models to describe the atomic composition of simple molecules and extended structures.

Grades 9–10 Science and Technical Subjects: Follow precisely a complex multistep procedure when carrying out experiments, taking measurements, or performing technical tasks, attending to special cases or exceptions defined in the text.

*(Continued)*

---

(Continued)

Grades 9–12 Science and Mathematics: Use mathematical representations to support the claim that the total momentum of a system of objects is conserved when there is no net force on the system.

Grade 11–12 Writing: Develop claim(s) and counterclaims fairly and thoroughly, supplying the most relevant data and evidence for each while pointing out the strengths and limitations of both claim(s) and counterclaims in a discipline-appropriate form that anticipates the audience's knowledge level, concerns, values, and possible biases.

*Source:* http://www.corestandards.org; http://www.nextgenscience.org.

Common Core as well as challenging new standards from discipline-based organizations (e.g., Next Generation Science Standards) indicate *what* to teach—the curriculum content—but not *how* to teach. What kind of instruction will help students achieve the kind of the intellectual rigor suggested in the standards?

Building on educational research since the late 1980s and more recent application of the research to professional development with more than 3,500 teachers in over 200 schools, the purpose of this book is twofold: to explain a well-researched instructional framework—we call it Authentic Intellectual Work (AIW)—that is consistent with, but not restricted to, the Common Core State Standards and to describe what we've learned about AIW implementation over 8 years of professional development with teachers and administrators using the framework to improve their instructional practice. The book offers no easy formula for transforming instruction. But reading and discussing it is a first step in an extended journey toward instruction grounded in intellectual rigor and relevance.

## ORGANIZATION

The book consists of several sections. Part I describes the AIW framework, its rationale, how it differs from common approaches to improve teaching, and a brief research summary of its contribution to student achievement. Part II uses classroom examples to show how the framework can be applied to analyze and improve teachers' lessons and assignments as well as student work. Each chapter highlights a different criterion of the framework and explains scoring the examples with the AIW standards for *construction of knowledge* (Chapter 2), *disciplined inquiry* (Chapter 3), and *value beyond school* (Chapter 4).

In Part III, Chapter 5 presents detailed research findings to offer further justification for teachers and administrators committing to professional development to improve instruction according to the AIW framework. Chapter 6 describes how schools can begin AIW professional development by addressing teachers' concerns in a couple of ways: committing to key organizational supports and embracing an approach to coaching teachers in teams that can build teachers' competence to use the AIW framework. Finally, Chapter 7 explains how leaders in districts, states, and other agencies can assist school teams in building and expanding teachers' capacity to promote students' Authentic Intellectual Work.

## AUDIENCE

The book is for educators who seek, through professional development, to improve the quality of instruction, assessment, and curriculum to ensure more rigorous and meaningful intellectual work for all students. The book should be useful to preK–12 teachers in all subjects and administrators in schools, districts, states, intermediate education agencies, and independent organizations involved in professional development who are considering investing in AIW. The text explains specific standards and rubrics to guide instruction in all subjects and grade levels, and makes specific recommendations for how to conduct effective professional development to enhance students' Authentic Intellectual Work. Those in leadership roles who make decisions about professional development, particularly while trying to implement Common Core or other national and state curriculum standards, should find it particularly useful.

Improving instruction through the AIW framework does not mean adopting yet another initiative disconnected from current practice or other reforms. Instead, the framework helps educators connect related reforms and reduce unnecessary initiatives to attain a rigorous and coherent instructional program. The AIW approach to improving instruction distinguishes itself in several ways from other initiatives:

1. It provides a common language for identifying intellectual rigor and relevance in any subject and grade level. This can guide instruction to implement the Common Core and other curricular ideals emphasizing complex intellectual work.

2. It does not prescribe use of specific instructional techniques such as cooperative group work, digital technology, or hands-on activities, but instead leaves such techniques up to the discretion of the teacher.

3. The standards for AIW and its approach to professional development support extensive teacher collaborative critical inquiry, which promotes school professional community that itself boosts student achievement.

4. The AIW framework and its approach to professional development are supported by multiyear research with large national samples and detailed case studies.

# Part I
## The AIW Framework

Students are more engaged and learn more when teachers challenge them to think critically, to delve deeply into problems and big ideas, and to make connections between their schoolwork and personal or real-world concerns. Unfortunately, education in the United States faces persistent obstacles that often undermine emphasis on rigorous intellectual work. These include low expectations for students to master intellectual challenge, especially for students from educationally disadvantaged backgrounds; lack of student engagement in academic work; and testing and curriculum demands for extensive content coverage and mastery of basic skills, instead of in-depth understanding of subject matter and complex communication skills. These obstacles, exacerbated by disagreement on education goals and the nature of effective instruction, along with diverse, ever-changing reform efforts, often leave teachers, administrators, parents, students, and the public at large without a clear sense of the intellectual mission of schooling.

Since the 1980s, national commissions composed of leading figures in public office, the business community, higher education, private foundations, and K–12 education have tried to address these issues through state and national standards for curriculum and assessment. Improvement has been demonstrated for some students in some subjects or grade levels in some districts and states, but on a national scale the movement toward standards has not significantly alleviated the main problems.

Beyond the obstacles just mentioned, successful education reform faces other roadblocks:

- The more recent standards movement for more rigorous intellectual work through the Common Core is vulnerable to disjointed implementation, inadequate funding, and further politicizing discourse on reform.

- Key educational leaders in schools, districts, and state and federal agencies usually commit to only short-term rather than sustained effort on promising initiatives.

- Key institutional actors (districts, states, unions, text and test publishers, and teacher training institutions) that influence classroom practices often fail to coordinate their programs, confounding teachers.

- And finally, resources are often distributed inequitably due to disparities in the power of different socioeconomic groups and to education funding based on property taxes.

Unless these social-political roadblocks are addressed more comprehensively, the standards movement alone is unlikely to improve schooling on a large scale. The work described here did not aim to resolve these more systemic problems.

Instead, the framework for Authentic Intellectual Work presented in Chapter 1 and elaborated throughout this book offers a parsimonious set of criteria and standards for rigorous, meaningful intellectual work that can focus instruction on a common intellectual mission for schooling across all grades and subjects. Professional development aimed to implement the framework helps teachers advance student mastery of more challenging curriculum specified in national and state standards. Chapter 1 defines Authentic Intellectual Work through specific criteria and examples, and offers a rationale for emphasizing it as the central intellectual mission of schooling.

# Chapter 1
## Authentic Intellectual Work

*Criteria, Examples, and Rationale*

**WHAT IS MEANINGFUL INTELLECTUAL WORK?**

What many students usually like about school is a favorite teacher, friends in class, or a particular subject they enjoy studying. When asked about the schoolwork itself, however, they rarely describe it as meaningful, significant, or worthwhile. Learning tasks often call for specific memorized information, retrieval of given information, or application of routine computational procedures, rather than higher-level thinking, interpretation, or in-depth conceptual understanding. Schoolwork can often be regarded largely as a series of contrived exercises necessary to earn credentials (grades, promotions) required for future success. When the challenge for students becomes figuring out how to comply with teachers' and tests' requirements, rather than using their minds to solve important meaningful problems or to answer interesting and challenging questions, this can increase disengagement and dropping out.

To define meaningful intellectual work with more specific criteria, we tried to identify the kinds of common mastery demonstrated by successful adults who continually work with knowledge, such as scientists, musicians, childcare workers, construction contractors, health care providers, business entrepreneurs, repair technicians, teachers, lobbyists, and citizen activists. Adults in these diverse endeavors face common intellectual challenges beyond mastery of basic information and skills to more complex academic work. These more complex common intellectual challenges can serve as guidelines for rigorous and meaningful education.

We do not expect children to achieve the same level of mastery accomplished by skilled adults, but identifying the commonalities in the intellectual work they do suggests criteria for intellectual performance necessary for success in contemporary society. Consider, for example, an engineer designing a bridge. To complete the bridge design successfully, the engineer relies on extensive factual knowledge from engineering, architecture, science, and mathematics. But the particular context for the bridge, such as its length, height, peak points of stress and load, the impact of local variation in weather, and other conditions, require the engineer to organize, analyze, and interpret all this background information to make a unique product. Consider also a citizen trying to make an informed decision about whether an elected officeholder has done a good enough job to be reelected over the challengers, or trying to make a convincing public statement to increase local funding for school security. Finally, consider a single parent of preschool children who calculates the costs and benefits of working outside the home, paying for childcare, and deciding how to choose among childcare providers. These examples illustrate how diverse endeavors in work, citizenship, and personal affairs present adults with intellectual challenges that differ from those commonly experienced by students in schools. Such challenges can serve as guidelines for curriculum, instruction, and assessment that extend beyond the basics and extensive lists of content standards to more complex intellectual work.

To signify the difference between the intellectual accomplishment of skilled adults and the typical work that students do in school, we refer to the more complex adult accomplishments as *Authentic Intellectual Work*. *Authentic* is used not to suggest that students are always unmotivated to succeed in conventional academic work, or that basic skills and proficiencies should be devalued, but to identify some kinds of intellectual work as more complex and more socially or personally meaningful. This enhanced complexity and meaning is grounded in original application of knowledge and skills (rather than just routine use of facts and procedures) in careful study of the details of a particular problem and in producing a product, service, or presentation that has meaning beyond success in school. We summarize these distinctive characteristics of Authentic Intellectual Work (AIW) as *construction of knowledge*, through the use of *disciplined inquiry*, to produce discourse, products, or performances that have *value beyond school*.

## AIW CRITERIA

### Construction of Knowledge

Skilled adults in diverse occupations and participating in civic life face the challenge of applying basic skills and knowledge to complex problems they have not previously faced. To reach adequate solutions to new problems, the competent adult has to "construct" knowledge because these problems cannot be solved by routine use of information or skills previously learned. Construction of knowledge involves organizing, interpreting, evaluating, or synthesizing prior knowledge to solve unique or novel problems. Teachers often think of these operations as higher order thinking skills. We contend, however, that construction of knowledge is best achieved not from explicit teaching of discrete "thinking skills" divorced from the problems' contexts. Instead success in construction of knowledge more often comes from tackling a variety of problems that can be successfully solved by doing this kind of cognitive work.

### Disciplined Inquiry

Constructing knowledge alone is not enough. The mere fact that someone has constructed, rather than reproduced, a solution to a problem is no guarantee that the solution is adequate or valid. Authentic adult intellectual accomplishments require that construction of knowledge be guided by disciplined inquiry. By this we mean that they (1) use a prior knowledge base often grounded in an academic or applied discipline, (2) strive for in-depth understanding rather than superficial awareness, and (3) develop and express their ideas and findings through elaborated communication.

*Prior knowledge base.* Significant intellectual accomplishments build on prior knowledge accumulated in an academic or applied discipline. Students must acquire a knowledge base of facts, vocabularies, concepts, theories, algorithms, and other methods and processes in the field necessary to conduct rigorous inquiry. Typical instruction is limited only to transmitting a knowledge base, along with basic skills, and neglects the following components of disciplined inquiry.

*In-depth understanding.* A useful knowledge base entails more than familiarity with facts, conventions, and skills in a broad range of topics. To be most powerful, the knowledge must extend beyond isolated facts and skills; it must be used to gain deep, complex understanding of specific problems. In-depth understanding develops as one uses the knowledge, concepts, methods, and processes of a discipline to look for, imagine, propose, and test relationships among key facts, events, concepts, rules, and claims to clarify a specific problem or issue.

*Elaborated communication.* Accomplished adults in diverse fields rely on complex forms of communication both to conduct their work and to present its results. The tools they use—verbal, symbolic, graphic, and visual—provide qualifications, nuances, elaborations, details, and analogies woven into extended narratives, explanations, justifications, and dialogue. Elaborated communication may be most often evident in essays or research papers, but a math proof, CAD drawing, complex display board, or musical score can also involve elaborated communication.

## Value Beyond School

Finally, meaningful intellectual accomplishments have utilitarian, aesthetic, or personal value. When adults write letters, news articles, organizational memos, or technical reports; when they speak a foreign language; when they design a house, negotiate an agreement, or devise a budget; when they create a painting or a piece of music—they try to communicate ideas that have an impact on others. In contrast, school assignments such as spelling quizzes, laboratory exercises, or typical final exams are usually designed only to document the learner's success in meeting the demands of the teacher; that is, they lack utilitarian, aesthetic, or personal meaning for the student or others beyond certifying the student's success in school.

Curriculum or instruction intended to be relevant, student-centered, hands-on, or activity-based may be construed as having value beyond school. But these labels alone do not necessarily represent the intellectual component in our concept of value beyond school. Intellectual challenges raised in the world beyond the classroom are often more meaningful to students than those contrived only for the purpose of instructing students in school. But the key here is to involve students in any activity—regardless of whether it conforms to familiar notions of relevance, student interest, or participatory learning—that presents an intellectual challenge which when successfully met, has meaning to students beyond complying with teachers' requirements.

The three criteria—*construction of knowledge,* through *disciplined inquiry,* to produce discourse, products, and performances that have meaning and *value beyond* success in *school*—provide the foundation or criteria for the more complex intellectual work necessary for success in contemporary society. While some people may regard the term *authentic* as equivalent to the criterion of value beyond school, this is only one component of Authentic Intellectual Work. All three criteria are important. For example, students might confront a complex calculus problem demanding analytic thought (construction of knowledge and disciplined inquiry), but if its solution has no interest or value beyond proving competence to pass a course, students are less likely be able to use the knowledge in their lives beyond school. Or a student might be asked to write a letter to the editor about a proposed social welfare policy. She might say she vigorously opposes the policy but offer no arguments indicating that she understands relevant economic and moral issues. This activity may meet the criteria of constructing knowledge to produce discourse with value beyond school, but it would fall short on the criterion of disciplined inquiry and thereby represent only superficial awareness, not deep understanding, of the issue. As a final example, students might be asked to interview family members about experiences during wartime or to conduct a survey of peer opinion on job conditions or musical preferences. These activities would connect schoolwork to students' lives beyond school, but if students only reported what the interviewees said, without summary or analysis or drawing connections to disciplinary content, there would be virtually no construction of knowledge or disciplined inquiry. Judgments about the extent to which intellectual work is authentic should be made on a continuum, from less to more, depending on how fully all three criteria are met and on expectations of mastery appropriate for different grade levels.

## EXAMPLES FROM THE FIELD

What does Authentic Intellectual Work by students look like? The following positive examples from different subjects and grade levels show students constructing knowledge through disciplined inquiry to produce intellectual work that has meaning and value beyond completing tasks in school. Each represents an individual student's unique work, not a restatement of work completed by all students in a class.[1] Following each positive example, a contrasting example is provided to illustrate student work that falls short on the three criteria.

Judgments about student success in meeting the criteria for Authentic Intellectual Work can be applied and compared most reliably if assignments call for student writing. For this reason, initial research on AIW concentrated on Grades 3 and above, where student writing is more common than in lower grades. Since 2007, when the AIW professional development initiative took off, we have found it possible to adapt the framework from pre-kindergarten on.

## Authentic Intellectual Work Example—Grade 3 Mathematics

**Assignment**: "We have been working on looking for clues in word problems all year. Let's take a look at these word problems. Let's read the directions. We know that these word problems will be either multiplication or division problems. Read the first problem silently. Look for a clue word or words that will tell you if this is multiplication or division. Do the number problems in the work space. Does this answer make sense? Underline any clue words that helped you decide on dividing or multiplying. Do the rest of the problems in this manner."

After checking the answers and discussing clue words, students were told: "Write five word problems of your own on a separate sheet of paper for homework. We will read these problems in class tomorrow, looking for clue words. If we hear your clue words and your problems make sense, you will win a prize (sticker)."

### Third-Grade Problem Solving

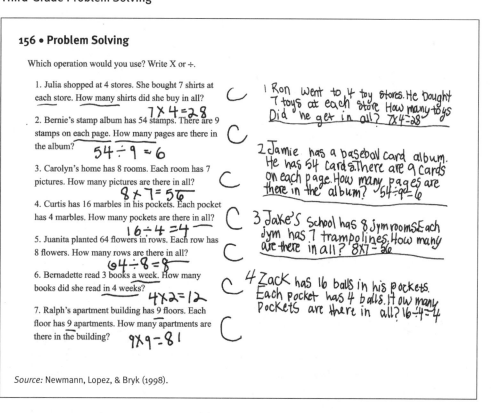

**156 • Problem Solving**

Which operation would you use? Write X or ÷.

1. Julia shopped at 4 stores. She bought 7 shirts at each store. How many shirts did she buy in all?
$7 \times 4 = 28$

2. Bernie's stamp album has 54 stamps. There are 9 stamps on each page. How many pages are there in the album?
$54 \div 9 = 6$

3. Carolyn's home has 8 rooms. Each room has 7 pictures. How many pictures are there in all?
$8 \times 7 = 56$

4. Curtis has 16 marbles in his pockets. Each pocket has 4 marbles. How many pockets are there in all?
$16 \div 4 = 4$

5. Juanita planted 64 flowers in rows. Each row has 8 flowers. How many rows are there in all?
$64 \div 8 = 8$

6. Bernadette read 3 books a week. How many books did she read in 4 weeks?
$4 \times 2 = 12$

7. Ralph's apartment building has 9 floors. Each floor has 9 apartments. How many apartments are there in the building?
$9 \times 9 = 81$

1 Ron went to 4 toy stores. He bought 7 toys at each store. How many toys Did he get in all? 7X4=28

2 Jamie has a baseball card album. He has 54 cards. There are 9 cards on each page. How many pages are there in the album? 54÷9=6

3 Jake's school has 8 jym rooms. Each jym has 7 trampolines. How many are there in all? 8X7=36

4 Zack has 16 balls in his pockets. Each pocket has 4 balls. How many pockets are there in all? 16÷4=4

*Source:* Newmann, Lopez, & Bryk (1998).

The student constructed knowledge by inventing word problems illustrating concepts of multiplication and division. Correct answers on the worksheet and in the student-constructed problems indicated understanding of the concepts, and the details offered in the word problems indicated elaborated writing. The problems posed by the student extended beyond the classroom and their solutions required application of mathematics.

## Contrasting Example—Grade 3 Mathematics

Assignment: We have been working on different ways to collect information about something. Another word for information is *data*. Last week we took a survey on the food choices for our spring picnic. Look at the results and answer the following questions:

---

**Third-Grade Food Tallies**

| Picnic choices | Votes |
|---|---|
| 1) Pizza | ~~卌~~ 卌 \|\|\| |
| 2) Hot dogs | 卌 卌 \|\| |
| 3) Sub Sandwiches | 卌 \| |
| 4) Sloppy Joes | \|\| |

- Which food got the least votes? *Sloppy Joes*
- Which food got the most votes? *Hot Dogs*
- How many votes did hot dogs get? *17*
- How many students, total, voted? *28*
- How many votes did your choice get? *9*

---

Instead of requiring students to construct mathematical knowledge, the lesson asked only that students reproduce information given in the chart. Though the students added tally marks to find totals on some questions, the work included no elaboration or explanation of answers. The picnic choices involved items of interest beyond the classroom, but the lesson did not ask students to use mathematics to solve a real-world problem.

## Authentic Intellectual Work Example—Grade 5 Language Arts

Students were instructed: "Write a fable. Choose two animal characters. Think of some advice that will work as the moral of a fable. Then write a short fable that illustrates the moral. The fable must include conversation (dialogue)."

## Fifth-Grade Fable

One student wrote the following:

---

**The Bear's Decision**

There once was a bear who ruled the forest of animals. He was looking for helpers to help him with the land's decisions. A dog, sparrow, rat and monkey became the bear's helpers.

One day a hyena came to the forest. He heard that the lord was looking for one more helper for the king. He went to the bear's castle. He spoke to the bear. He said, "Is it true that you seek help to govern the land?" The bear said, "You have heard correctly." The hyena then said, "You must let me become your helper, because if you don't, I will destroy you, and I will become king!" The bear, upset about the hyena said, "You think I'm scared? Guards, take this lunatic away from my sight! He does not deserve anything for threatening me!" That was what the guards did.

A cat also heard of this and spoke to the king. The cat told the king he was without a job because he was blamed of something he didn't do. The cat said, "I have looked for jobs, only to find nothing. I will be of use for the rest of your life. " The bear said, "You are noble and good. You will become my helper. "

The hyena heard of the cat. He learned this lesson too late. Persuasion is better than getting what you want through force.

*Source:* Newmann et al. (1998).

---

By inventing and organizing the story's different parts, the student constructed knowledge. The coherently developed details of the story illustrate elaborated writing and in-depth understanding of the concept of fable and moral lesson of a fable. The intellectual work was directed to a persistent problem relevant to the lives of students and others outside of school—the use of force versus reason to solve problems.

## Contrasting Example—Grade 5 Language Arts/Social Studies

Assignment: Make a travel brochure. Be sure to include your name and date on the brochure and do quality work when including the following contents:

- a colorful cover that illustrates and labels a landmark or landform from that place
- a colorful and labeled map of the place
- a list of four interesting facts
- an itinerary with five interesting activities for your travelers to do at different locations
- a packing list
- a choice page with your own ideas

Galapagos Tour Brochure

# THE GALAPAGOS ISLANDS

By: Arlo Fifth Grader

## Let's start out with some basic facts.

About 150 species of bird thrive on the Galapagos Islands. About on earth.

**#1.** Over 150 species of bird thrive on the Galapagos Islands. They are found nowhere else on earth. They are green half of them can be found underwater just to eat green half of them can be found underwater on earth.

**#2.** Marine sea iguanas live on the Galapagos Islands. They will dive 30 feet underwater to be strong swimmers. They are the only sea lizards on earth. They are thought to be strong swimmers. They are the only sea lizards on earth.

**#3.** The oldest islands in the Galapagos Islands are only and a half million years old. Yet the youngest is only about seven hundred thousand.

**#4.** There are only five places in the Galapagos Islands that are about seven hundred thousand. Everywhere else animals roam freely. There are only five places in the Galapagos Islands that are inhabited by humans. Everywhere else animals roam freely.

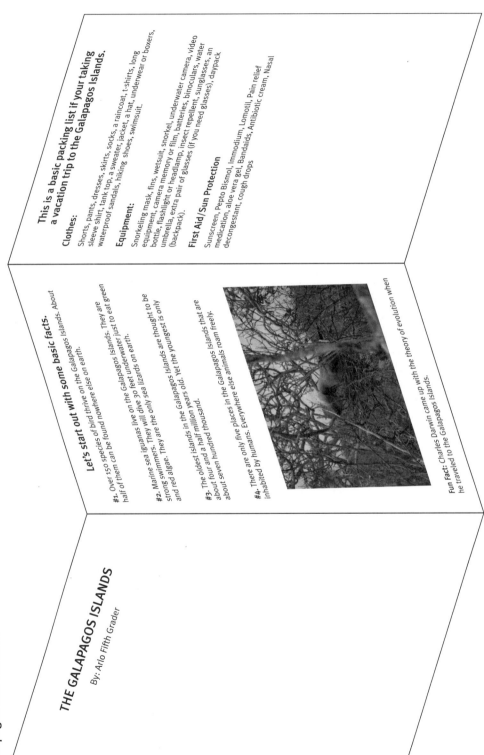

**Fun Fact:** Charles Darwin came up with the theory of evolution when he traveled to the Galapagos Islands.

## This is a basic packing list if your taking a vacation trip to the Galapagos Islands.

### Clothes:

Shorts, pants, dresses, skirts, socks, a raincoat, t-shirts, long sleeve shirt, tank top, a sweater, jacket, a hat, underwear or boxers, waterproof Sandals, hiking shoes, swimsuit.

### Equipment:

Snorkeling mask, fins, wetsuit, snorkel, underwater camera, video equipment, camera memory or film, batteries, binoculars, video bottle, flashlight or headlamp, insect repellent, sunglasses, water umbrella, extra pair of glasses (if you need glasses), daypack (backpack).

### First Aid/Sun Protection

Sunscreen, Pepto Bismol, Immodium, Lomotil, Pain relief medication, aloe vera gel, Bandaids, Antibiotic cream, Nasal decongestant, cough drops

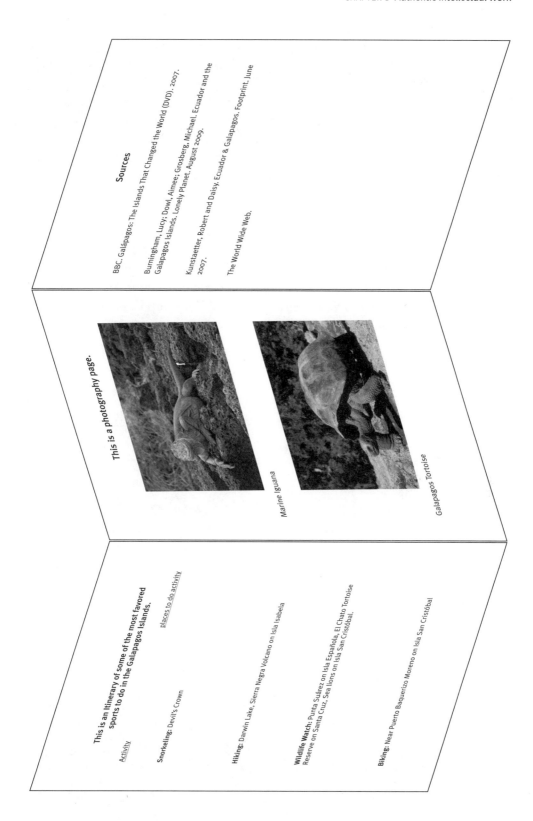

**Sources**

BBC. Galápagos: The Islands That Changed the World (DVD). 2007.

Burningham, Lucy; Dowl, Aimee; Grosberg, Michael. Ecuador and the Galapagos Islands. Lonely Planet. August 2009.

Kunstaetter, Robert and Daisy. Ecuador & Galapagos. Footprint. June 2007.

The World Wide Web.

*This is a photography page.*

Marine Iguana

Galápagos Tortoise

**This is an itinerary of some of the most favored sports to do in the Galapagos Islands.**

Activity                    places to do activity

**Snorkeling:** Devil's Crown

**Hiking:** Darwin Lake., Sierra Negra Volcano on Isla Isabela

**Wildlife Watch:** Punta Suárez on Isla Española, El Chato Tortoise Reserve on Santa Cruz, Sea lions on Isla San Cristóbal.

**Biking:** Near Puerto Baquerizo Moreno on Isla San Cristóbal

Students might enjoy creating their own travel brochures, but the assignment does not require construction of knowledge. Instead, this student simply retrieved information from other sources and reproduced it in the brochure. Neither does the assignment demand disciplined inquiry; there is no elaboration or argument as to why someone should travel to their location and no evidence of conceptual understanding of Darwin's theory of evolution or the connection between items in the packing list and the climate or geography of the Galapagos. The assignment does pose a problem that can have value beyond school, that is, designing a travel brochure to an interesting place. But it still scores low on this criterion, because the assignment fails to require application of key concepts or processes in the disciplines of language arts or social studies necessary to solve travel-related problems or create an effective brochure.

## Authentic Intellectual Work Example—Grade 12 History

Students were instructed to develop a position paper on a controversial issue. The following excerpts are from one student's longer essay justifying U.S. intervention in Kuwait in the Persian Gulf in 1991.

## Twelfth-Grade Essay

---

**A Time for War**

There have been numerous instances when the world has witnessed what happens when aggressors are not stopped. Let us look back to 1935 when Mussolini decided to invade and annex Ethiopia. Ethiopia's emperor appealed to the League of Nations, but nothing was done.

Soon afterwards, in 1936, Adolph Hitler reoccupied the Rhineland, thereby violating the Treaty of Versailles. Again, the world ignored these blatant displays of hostility and power . . .

When Emperor Hirohito of Japan attacked Manchuria in 1931, and then China in 1937, he was simply scolded by the League of Nations...

In 1938, Hitler united Austria and Germany. The world protested, but then gave in to Hitler who said he only wanted to unite the German people. Then, Hitler took the Sudentenland from Czechoslovakia. As before, concessions were made to appease the aggressor . . .

In all the examples of unchecked aggression, the moral is the same. The school bully who demands lunch money from other children will not stop until someone stands up to him. If the bully is allowed to harass, intimidate, and steal from other children, it is giving him silent permission to use power against the weak...

Those who complain about the United States acting as a "police nation" would do well to remember that Desert Storm has been a United Nations effort, not solely a U.S. effort. The U.N. Security Council condemned Iraq's invasion and annexation of Kuwait, as did the Arab League. The U.N. imposed mandatory sanctions, forbidding all member states from doing business with Iraq. The European Community, the United States and Japan froze Kuwaiti assets. The United

---

States, Britain, France, Canada, Australia, West Germany, the Netherlands, and Belgium; acted in accordance with the United Nations and with the support of its many members.

There is a time for peace and a time for war. War is a horrible situation, but it is imperative that countries learn to recognize when it is necessary. Perhaps someday the world will be able to solve its problems without violence. In the meantime, we would endanger international security to allow people like Saddam Hussein and his terrorist goons to threaten and overpower independent countries such as Kuwait.

*Source:* Newmann et al. (1995).

By organizing an argument for intervention to stop international aggression, especially when international support for the intervention is evident, the student constructed knowledge. Elaboration was offered by citing historical instances in which aggression, if not stopped, led to a chain of negative consequences. In addressing an important policy issue of the day, the student produced intellectual work connected to issues beyond school.

## Contrasting Example—Grade 12 Government

Weekly assignment: Following current events is a key part of being an informed citizen. Throughout the semester, you are required to complete weekly "current event sheets" as evidence that you are reading the paper or online sources. The format is consistent from week to week, but you can choose your news.

**Sunday Sports**

## Current Events

NAME: Gina

HOUR: 2

DATE: 4/7/2015

SOURCE: NY TIMES

1. WHO, WHAT, WHERE, WHEN, WHY? SUMMARIZE IN 3-4 SENTENCES. WHAT IS THE CURRENT EVENT ABOUT?

*Derrick Gordon admitted he was gay a year ago, which is hard to do because he's an athlete in Indiana. Especially being apart of the sports community, where LGBT issues are being supported by them.*

*(Continued)*

---

(Continued)

2. **HOW DOES THIS CURRENT EVENT RELATE TO YOU? THIS SECTION SHOULE BE 1-2 SENTENCES.** 1 point

   *Because it's important to accept people who are gay because it's ~~how~~ who they are.*

3. **WHY DID YOU PICK THIS CURRENT EVENT? WHY WAS IT INTERESTING TO YOU? THIS SECTION SHOULD BE 2-3 SENTENCES.** 1.5 points

   *I like sports and am concerned about the rights of all individuals.*

---

This student's work shows no construction of knowledge, only retrieving information from the newspaper (question 1) or reporting personal experiences or feelings about the article (questions 2 and 3). While questions 2 and 3 could have asked students to use disciplined inquiry by elaborating on reasons for their choices and explaining the choices with key ideas in the study of government/civics (e.g., the role of government and other organizations in promoting equality and reducing discrimination), they did not. Finally, although the student chose to summarize news on an important civic problem beyond school—the extent to which gays experience discrimination and equal treatment—the assignment scores low on value beyond school, because it failed to require application of disciplined knowledge to address a problem beyond school.

## RATIONALE: WHY SHOULD SCHOOLS PROMOTE AUTHENTIC INTELLECTUAL WORK?

Schools are called upon to serve a myriad of purposes: teaching basic skills in literacy and mathematics, preparing students for higher education and democratic civic participation, encouraging responsible social behavior, celebrating cultural diversity, providing information on health and consumer success, and developing workplace technical and human relations skills. These purposes all seem legitimate, but educators and students alike can feel overwhelmed by the voluminous agenda, especially when topics, standards, and courses are taught as separate, unconnected items. There is usually so much material to cover in a limited time that students and teachers rarely have opportunities to reflect carefully on what they are learning.

Does Authentic Intellectual Work represent yet an additional task on an already overcrowded agenda? Promoting Authentic Intellectual Work should not be seen as adding a new or different educational goal. Instead, AIW provides a framework for teaching and assessing any goal that relies on knowledge from an academic or applied discipline. The framework does not prescribe how schools should arrive at priorities among the many tasks they are asked to perform. These issues must be resolved through democratic processes in communities, states, and the federal system. The framework does, however, clarify how teachers can design instruction and assessment in academic or applied disciplines to include assignments and activities that truly foster student opportunities to produce Authentic Intellectual Work.

The AIW framework focuses on only one aspect of teaching: authentic intellectual quality. As such, it does not address many other issues important to teachers. A more complete look at the quality of instruction and assessment would probably also address what specific curriculum content to include, how to achieve coherence among daily lessons that connect to a larger unit of study and to other grade levels, and how to accomplish other above-mentioned educational goals that, while legitimate, often override attention to intellectual quality. Focusing systematically on intellectual rigor as defined by the criteria for Authentic Intellectual Work will

- prepare students for the intellectual demands of the workplace, citizenship, and personal affairs;

- increase student engagement in learning;

- strengthen school professional community; and

- boost student achievement.

## Preparing for the Intellectual Demands of the Workplace, Citizenship, and Personal Affairs

Studies of cognitive demands in modern workplaces document the importance of workers' problem-solving skills, in-depth understanding of problems and specific vocational content on the job, and elaborated nuanced forms of communication (Cappelli et al., 1997; Decker, Rice, Moore, & Rollefson, 1997; Murnane & Levy, 1996; National Center on Education and the Economy, 1990). While millions of jobs continue to require only low-level skills, as a matter of fairness all students deserve the opportunity to be educated for the demands of intellectually challenging workplaces.

Public investment in education is justified, not only for its contribution to individual economic success but also for building civic competence and skills in managing personal affairs. From Aristotle to Jefferson to Dewey to contemporary political scientists, the argument for democracy assumes that citizens are capable not only of basic literacy but also of exercising principled and reasoned judgment about public affairs (Aristotle, 1946; Barber, 1984; Dewey, 1916/1966; Jefferson, 1939). Students arriving at defensible positions on controversial public issues—from local disposal of toxic waste to national regulation of campaign financing, from deciding whether to support a school referendum to considering whether to vote for a candidate who most consistently agrees with your positions but is not likely to win, to how to best to allocate scarce personal time to participate in local volunteer organizations—all require interpretation, evaluation, in-depth understanding, and elaborated communication that extends well beyond traditional tests of knowledge.

Finally, education should reinforce the intellectual competence needed to maximize individual health, safety, and personal fulfillment. Consider the intellectual competence required in contemporary society to care for one's family and friends, to be safe and maintain health, to manage one's time and resources, and to develop rewarding hobbies and relationships. Coping with escalating and often conflicting information in each of these areas presents daunting challenges of interpretation, analysis, and synthesis; in-depth understanding of specific problems; and work with elaborate forms of written, oral, and electronic communication.

## Increasing Student Engagement in Learning

Participation in authentic intellectual activity is more likely to motivate and sustain students in the hard work that learning requires. Teachers report that Authentic Intellectual Work is often more interesting and meaningful to students than repeated drills aimed at disconnected knowledge and skills. Almost 50% of high school dropouts leave because school is not interesting for them, and nearly 70% say they are not motivated to work hard (Bridgeland, DiIulio, & Morison, 2006). Research indicates that students exposed to authentic intellectual challenges are more engaged in their schoolwork than students exposed to more conventional schoolwork. (For evidence of the connection between Authentic Intellectual Work and student engagement, see Avery, 1999; Kane, Khattri, Reeve, Adamsom, & Pelavin Research Institute, 1995; Marks, 2000; Newmann, Marks, & Gamoran, 1996.)

When students have opportunities to construct knowledge rather than only reproduce what they have been given, to understand topics in depth instead of only superficially, to express themselves by explaining their ideas, and to study topics that have some significance beyond the classroom, they are more likely to care about and be interested in learning and willing to devote the serious effort that learning requires. Increased opportunities for student engagement offered through Authentic Intellectual Work may make schooling more "fun," but what counts is that the increased engagement increases student effort, which pays off in higher student achievement on both basic skills and more complex intellectual challenges.

## Strengthening School Professional Community

The criteria for Authentic Intellectual Work, along with the more specific standards presented in Chapters 2, 3, and 4, provide a common professional language for teachers and administrators to define the intellectual mission of the school, which helps in selection of curricular content as well as instructional and student assessments. By defining the kinds of intellectual work to be nurtured in common across subjects and grade levels, this framework transcends lists of specific content and skills particular to different subjects and grade levels, thereby strengthening unity on the academic purpose within a school.[2]

The criteria and specific standards for evaluating instruction and student work stimulate teacher dialogue and cooperative planning within and across grade levels and subjects. And these efforts in turn bring coherence to teaching and learning, whether the school is engaged in Common Core implementation, technology integration, professional learning communities, data-driven decision making, or other efforts to improve. Because the dialogue is grounded in intellectual activities systematically applied across grades and subjects, the framework becomes more meaningful than school missions expressed only in vague slogans, such as "success for all students" or "proficiency in each content area," or missions that specify discrete content and skill mastery for each grade but offer no transcending explicit intellectual goals. Furthermore, unlike reform efforts that favor subject areas tied only to state-level standardized tests or that minimize academics to focus on behavior programs, AIW reform allows every teacher in any subject to increase the level of rigor and meaningful learning in class. When the schoolwide mission for learning is clarified, teachers' collaboration can focus on teaching skills and content in their areas according to the criteria for Authentic Intellectual Work.

## Boosting Student Achievement

Evidence that AIW instruction boosts student achievement further justifies using the AIW framework to guide teaching and learning. The evidence comes from two types of research.[3] First, from 1990 to 2011, several studies measured the extent to which observed instruction and assessment reflected AIW standards and found a strong connection. In hundreds of schools in different communities throughout world with diverse student populations in Grades 3–12, and in the subjects of mathematics, social studies, language arts, and science, these studies showed tremendous achievement advantages for all students (regardless of gender, race, or socioeconomic status) whose teachers made higher demands for Authentic Intellectual Work. On both conventional standardized tests and more authentic assessments of student achievement, students with teachers who scored high on AIW criteria scored higher than students whose teachers scored low on AIW standards. These initial studies, however, examined teaching as it occurred naturally, without teachers being aware of the AIW standards or having professional development to promote them.

By 2007, after several studies on existing practice in different contexts showed strong relationships between authentic instruction and student achievement, we concluded that teachers and students could benefit from professional development to help teachers deliberately teach according to the AIW framework. Thus began the Iowa project and professional development in other contexts described in this book. By 2011 it was possible to begin the second research stage; that is, to examine the extent to which professional development to implement AIW standards boosts student achievement. This initial evaluation examined achievement results of the project in Iowa for 16 schools, in 10 districts, in which all teachers engaged in AIW as their primary professional development for one full year prior to the date of testing in 2010–2011. These districts and schools were compared with another set of matched Iowa schools and districts not implementing AIW. Achievement was measured by the standardized 2010–2011 Iowa Tests of Basic Skills (ITBS; Grades 3–8) and Iowa Tests of Educational Development (IETD; Grades 9–11).

Students in AIW schools across grade levels and subjects scored higher on the ITBS and ITED than students in non-AIW schools. AIW schools also had higher percentages of students scoring proficient. Beyond the benefits to student achievement, the initial evaluation found that AIW professional development improved teachers' practice (e.g., teachers' assignments improved according to AIW standards) and improved school culture (e.g., teachers and administrators noticed increased cooperative, collaborative teacher planning).

## SUMMARY

In this chapter we described the need for student involvement in more rigorous and meaningful intellectual work and explained that national curriculum standards toward this end must be supplemented by appropriate instructional standards, which we proposed as the basis of the Authentic Intellectual Work framework. Three main criteria— *construction of knowledge*, through the use of *disciplined inquiry*, to produce discourse, products, or performances that have *value beyond school*—define the AIW framework and were illustrated by considering samples of student work in different grade levels and subjects. Using the framework to guide teaching in all subjects and grade levels was justified for helping students resolve intellectual challenges posed by work, citizenship, and personal affairs; increasing student engagement in learning; strengthening school professional community; and boosting student achievement. The chapter offered a foundation for professional development, described more fully in chapters to follow, to help teachers implement the framework.

# Part II
## Teaching to Promote Authentic Intellectual Work
### *Criteria, Standards, and Rubrics*

In Part I we described examples of adults engaged in Authentic Intellectual Work (AIW). In what ways might teachers promote Authentic Intellectual Work among students? As with many other ideas and slogans that capture public attention, educators have diverse and vague notions of "authentic" education. At a recent national staff development conference, we heard the term used frequently yet rarely explained in ways that carried useful implications for how to improve instruction. Some common questions raised at the conference illustrated confusion on how to apply the term, for example: "Isn't all learning in schools authentic, since students will use it at some point in their lives?" "For education to be authentic, must all traditional teaching be abandoned?" "If a teacher describes only a 'real-world' application of material learned, is that enough to make the work authentic?" Such questions call for a specific and clear definition of Authentic Intellectual Work in schools.

We summarize the three distinctive criteria of Authentic Intellectual Work as *construction of knowledge*, through the use of *disciplined inquiry*, to produce discourse, products, or performances that have *value beyond school*. Part I provided an overview and a summary of the research supporting these three features. The purpose of Part II is to provide concrete examples of each of these criteria of Authentic Intellectual Work in schools a along with standards and rubrics that further define the criteria to help teachers plan lessons, create assignments, and analyze student work. Chapters 3, 4, and 5 present actual high-scoring examples of lessons, assignments for students, and student work scored according to standards and rubrics for each of the three criteria. Explanations for the scores on the rubrics show how the examples meet the criteria and standards.

The standards for AIW, and the chapters in Part II, are organized according to the three main criteria. As indicated in Table 1, the wording of specific standards for each criterion varies somewhat for instruction, tasks, and student performance. Standards for *construction of knowledge* and *disciplined inquiry* place special emphasis on higher order thinking, cognitive complexity, and teaching for understanding. Activities scoring high on *value beyond school* must indicate that students are challenged to transfer and apply academic understanding to address issues or problems in the world beyond school. The meanings of standards summarized in the table are clarified further in the chapters to follow.

**Table 1  Framework for Authentic Intellectual Work**

| Criteria | Standards | | |
|---|---|---|---|
| | Instruction (lessons taught) | Tasks (assignments, assessments) | Student performance (student work) |
| **Construction of knowledge** | Higher Order Thinking | Construction of Knowledge | Construction of Knowledge |
| **Disciplined inquiry** | Deep Knowledge and Student Understanding | | Conceptual Understanding |
| | Substantive Conversation | Elaborated Communication | Elaborated Communication |
| **Value beyond school** | Value Beyond School | Value Beyond School | *(Student performance is not scored on this standard)* |

Each chapter focuses on a different criterion in the framework by considering tasks, student performance, and instruction that meet the criterion to a high degree. Chapter 5 concludes with an example to demonstrate a task that scores at the highest level for all three standards. Across Chapters 2, 3, and 4, we include artifacts that represent a range of grade levels and subject areas.

We use the term *artifact* when referring to examples of instruction, tasks, and student performance. An artifact for tasks includes any important assignment teachers ask students to complete, such as homework, tests, labs, projects, or reports using digital technology. The work that students produce when completing a task could include artifacts such as essays, digital presentations, graphs, art, or video of actual performances. Descriptions of lessons, or videos thereof, can serve as artifacts of instruction and could include documentation of student dialogue, small-group instruction activity, simulations, or summaries of direct instruction. When scoring instruction on an AIW team, the lesson should be either observed live or viewed on video. Here, however, we use text descriptions of lessons to examine how the standards can be applied to an instructional context.

Teachers typically use rubrics for specific assessments to identify the knowledge and skills for different levels of proficiency in a subject at a given grade level and to help assign a grade to student work. While these are important, the main objective of the AIW standards and rubrics is to promote instructional improvement and coherence across all subjects and grades. Since rubrics in the AIW framework are used across subject areas and grade levels and are designed to identify general qualities of high-quality, rigorous academic work, they do not prescribe the content to be taught or the extent to which the content of any lesson, assignment, or piece of student work is sufficiently authoritative or accurate. Such judgments are best left to the professional discretion of teachers and others with knowledge of the relevant discipline and grade level. As AIW implementation proceeds in a school, teachers will need to determine for each assignment or piece of student work whether the knowledge and skills called for and demonstrated are appropriate and acceptable.

As an introduction to the scoring process, these chapters reflect the foundation for critical inquiry that the AIW standards support when teachers meet in teams. To illustrate the AIW criteria, we present and discuss only high-scoring artifacts. In actual team meetings, teachers bring artifacts that need improvement, and colleagues use the scoring discussion to provide feedback aimed at elevating AIW standards. The beginning of each chapter includes a brief discussion of the essence of that chapter's criterion. However, once a school begins professional development to teach for AIW and to make its discussions and scoring align with the AIW criteria, teachers will need the full set of rubrics and scoring guidelines presented in *Teaching for Authentic Intellectual Work: Standards and Scoring Criteria for Teachers' Tasks, Student Performance, and Instruction* (Newmann, King, & Carmichael, 2009). Chapters 2, 3, and 4 explain how high-scoring examples of instruction, tasks, and student performance are scored using criteria, standards, and rubrics in the scoring manual. Some examples in these chapters include the entire rubric, but others include only scoring rules for higher levels of the rubric. Still other examples may include criteria for much lower scores in order to show stark contrast.

The AIW criteria, standards, and rubrics offer a clear conception of rigorous teaching and learning that advances equity and excellence in student achievement. The framework provides a common language for instructional improvement, but the conversations among teachers and administrators in a school are critical to generating a collective understanding of the framework across the staff and to generating action steps for what they can do to increase academic and intellectual rigor. These conversations put teeth into professional development for continuous improvement; schools that cannot find the time to have sustained conversations will not be successful.

The goal of AIW implementation is for learning activities to score high a reasonable amount of the time regardless of students' ability levels. Ideally, we should have similar high standards and expectations for all learners, with modifications, adaptations, and scaffolding to help students who struggle with learning. AIW scoring involves taking the grade level into account (for example, elaborated communication looks different at the primary and secondary levels), but we must guard against dumbing down expectations because of some students' skill levels.

The instructional climate in a school should communicate high expectations for all students and should cultivate, through teachers and student peers, enough trust and respect to reward serious intellectual effort. For example, mistakes should be treated as opportunities for positive growth, not as occasions for negative judgments of personal worth. Meeting these standards demands consistent classroom support for all students to master challenging work. How teachers use these standards to guide professional development and critical inquiry in planning, teaching, and evaluation of practice is discussed in Part III.

# Chapter 2
## Construction of Knowledge

**OVERVIEW**

For many teachers, student thinking is fundamental to their pedagogy, and yet there are numerous interpretations, without consensus about what high-quality thinking looks like. The Authentic Intellectual Work (AIW) standard for *construction of knowledge* provides a definition of higher-level thinking useful to teachers of different grade levels and disciplines. *Construction of knowledge* is broadly determined by examining the degree to which teachers ask students to organize, interpret, analyze, synthesize, or evaluate information. Common applications include thinking about a concept, procedure, or problem, rather than retrieving or reporting information as previously given, or repeatedly applying previously learned procedures, facts, or definitions. A key distinction between our conception and other discussions of higher order thinking is that we emphasize that demands for any one of these cognitive operations (organize, interpret, analyze, synthesize, and evaluate information) signify an expectation of construction of knowledge because each is a departure from reproducing information as is customary in tasks that ask students only to state previously learned information, definitions, rules, and procedures. There is no order of preference, or hierarchy, given to the type of higher order thinking students engage in, just whether it is present. Often, complex tasks demand multiple operations in student thinking. In the discussion of evidence during an AIW team scoring session, however, teachers may address the nature of the thinking and suggest for example, that a focus on synthesis be preceded by a deeper analysis or that what students are being asked to organize could be enriched by adding interpretation.

Although the research on AIW focused on language arts, mathematics, science, and social studies, teachers interested in applying the AIW standards to other subjects can also use the standards, criteria, and scoring rules as appropriate for those subjects. Prior to the scoring process, scorers should attempt to identify and list as part of their scoring guidelines illustrative indicators of task demands for students to organize, interpret, analyze, synthesize, or evaluate information in the subject being scored.

**EXEMPLARS FROM THE FIELD**

To help illustrate how scoring can be applied to both core and non-core subjects, this chapter includes artifacts from different contexts, including a second-grade math assignment, a junior high school Spanish task, student work of high school chemistry, and a third-grade science lesson. Each artifact features strong use of *construction of knowledge.* The chapter presents an explanation of each standard, the rubric for scoring, the artifact to be scored, the assigned score, and an explanation for the score.

## Mathematical Tasks — Standard 1: Construction of Knowledge

> *Standard Summary: The task asks students to organize, interpret, analyze, synthesize, or evaluate information in addressing a mathematical theorem, concept, procedure, or problem, rather than to retrieve or report information as previously given or to repeatedly apply previously learned algorithms, definitions, rules, and procedures.*

Demands for any *one* of these cognitive operations (organize, interpret, analyze, synthesize, and evaluate information) signifies an expectation of construction of knowledge because each is a departure from reproducing information as is customary in tasks that ask students only to state previously learned information, algorithms, definitions, rules, and procedures.

### Construction of Knowledge Rubric for Mathematical Tasks[1]

| Score | Criteria |
| --- | --- |
| 3 | The task's dominant expectation is for students to organize, interpret, analyze, synthesize, or evaluate mathematical information rather than merely reproduce information. |
| 2 | There is some expectation for students to organize, interpret, analyze, synthesize, or evaluate mathematical information rather than merely reproduce information. |
| 1 | There is very little or no expectation for students to organize, interpret, analyze, synthesize, or evaluate mathematical information. The dominant expectation is for students to retrieve or reproduce fragments of knowledge or to repeatedly apply previously learned algorithms, definitions, rules, and procedures. |

### Example 1 of a Task: Second-Grade Math

At the beginning of second grade, Ms. Gilbert provides students with 20 tickets and a map of the fairgrounds. The tickets may be used to do anything they want at the fair, but students have time to do only four activities and they should use all 20 tickets. A map of the fair, with all the activities and required number of tickets per activity, is shown in Figure 2.1. Once students have selected their four activities, they write each in a box and include the required number of tickets on the corresponding line below the activity (see Figure 2.2). The sum of their number sentence should equal 20. Finally, students write a sentence telling which addition strategy they used to arrive at the sum.[2]

**Figure 2.1  Addville County Fair Map**

**Figure 2.2  Fun at the Fair Assignment Sheet**

## Score and Explanation

This assignment scores 3 on *construction of knowledge* because the task's dominant expectation is for students to analyze the mathematical information and develop specific solutions based on the information provided. Considering four activities makes the possible combinations more complex for a typical second grader, especially since there are no restrictions on repeating activities. With more than 15 possible correct combinations and over 50 incorrect ones, students must problem solve to develop mathematically correct solutions. They have to decide among several choices which activities they would like to do and analyze the cost of each ride and how it impacts their ability to afford the other activities they selected. Furthermore, the task requires students to develop an equation (called the "addition sentence") that shows how they reached a sum of 20; it also requires students to write a sentence that describes which addition strategy they used to arrive at the sum. In short, students analyze the activities, evaluate their selections using mathematics, and verify using mathematics that their selections can be justified by writing a mathematical sentence. This is a strong and age appropriate example of *construction* of *knowledge* in mathematics at the second-grade level.

## Example 2 of a Task: Middle School Spanish

In this assignment, Ms. Doll, a junior high school Spanish teacher, asked her students to create posters of a real or imaginary trip. The assignment lets them select five photos and describe everything they can about what happened the day each photo was taken. The assignment spans one week, and students are required to produce a draft and consult with the teacher. Effort, ability, and competence are all part of the grade. See Figure 2.3 for the entire task.

**Figure 2.3  Mis Vacaciones**

---

**Objetivo:** Describe un(os) viaje(s) que hiciste.

*Describe a trip that you went on.*[3]

**Proyecto:** Haz un póster que describe un viaje verdadero o imaginario que hiciste. Debes incluír por lo menos cinco fotos. Debes escribir todo lo que puedes de lo que pasó el día de la foto. Habilidad y esfuerzo son partes de la nota. ¡Impresióname! Muéstrame la primera copia (rough draft) cuando la termines.

*Make a poster that describes a real or imaginary trip that you went on. You should include at least five photos. You should write everything you can about what happened on the day of that photo. Ability/competence and effort are parts of your grade. Impress me! Show me the rough draft when you finish.*

**Tiempo:** Vas a tener una semana para hacer el póster. Debes trabajar en la primera copia del póster primero. Puedes diseñar el póster y arreglar las fotos mientras esperas hablar conmigo sobre la primera copia del póster.

*You will have one week to do the poster. You should work on the rough draft of the poster first. You can create the poster and organize the photos while you wait to speak with me about the rough draft of the poster.*

---

*Score and Explanation*[4]

This assignment scores 3 on *construction of knowledge* because the task's dominant expectation is for students to create a description for each of the five photos. We also know that each poster is unique because the directions allow students to use a real or imagined vacation. Students completing this assignment are not native Spanish speakers, so developing unique explanations in Spanish would require them to analyze the photos and create possible explanations for what could have happened or what did happen. The directions encourage students to expand and elaborate on their explanations, enhancing the creativity and original thinking. Even for those students who choose to retell events that happened, those events and explanations would be unique to each student's poster and not a replication of what happened in class. Another consideration that supports a high score is the amount of time students are given to complete the assignment. Given one week, students are able to use their creativity and look up words they may not have known or check grammar and spelling with their teacher. The assignment's requiring nonnative speakers to organize ideas in a foreign language indicates a strong example of *construction of knowledge* in Spanish at the middle school or junior high school level.

## Student Performance in Science—Standard 1: Construction of Knowledge

*Standard Summary: Student performance demonstrates thinking with scientific content by using interpretation, analysis, synthesis, or evaluation to construct knowledge, rather than merely retrieving or restating scientific facts, definitions, and scientific laws or repeatedly applying algorithms given by the teacher or other sources.*

Possible indicators of scientific interpretation, analysis, synthesis, or evaluation are students' hypothesizing, describing patterns, making models or simulations, building scientific arguments, or deciding among or inventing procedures. To score high on this standard, students' work must appear reasonably original, not merely a restatement of knowledge previously given in a text or discussion. If students' work includes only brief answers, but not notes, outlines, computations, or other indications of how they arrived at the answers, correct answers alone can indicate *construction of knowledge* if the scorer concludes that the scientific task could be completed successfully only if the student had engaged in *construction of knowledge.* According to this rule, even if students do not show how they arrived at answers, the work may still receive a 3 or 4 for *construction of knowledge.*

**Construction of Knowledge Rubric for Student Work in Science**

| Score | Criteria |
|---|---|
| 4 | Almost all of the student's work shows scientific interpretations, analysis, or evaluation. |
| 3 | A moderate, yet significant, portion of the student's work shows scientific interpretations, analysis, or evaluation. |
| 2 | A small portion of the student's work shows scientific interpretations, analysis, or evaluation. |
| 1 | Little or none of the student's work shows scientific interpretations, analysis, or evaluation. |

## Example of Student Work: High School Chemistry

For the first formal lab report in a high school chemistry class, Mr. Muyskens has students design an experiment to determine whether the crown given to their group is pure aluminum. The focus of this analysis is the student work, but the reader needs to see the task to understand the assignment. The complete assignment and a sample of corresponding student work are shown in Figure 2.4.

**Figure 2.4 The King's Crown Chemistry**

---

**Assignment**

In the first century BC the Roman architect Vitruvius related a story of how Archimedes uncovered a fraud in the manufacture of a golden crown commissioned by Hiero II, the king of Syracuse. The crown would have been in the form of a wreath. Hiero would have placed such a wreath on the statue of a god or goddess. Suspecting that the goldsmith might have replaced some of the gold given to him by an equal weight of silver, Hiero asked Archimedes to determine whether the wreath was pure gold. And because the wreath was a holy object dedicated to the gods, he could not disturb the wreath in any way. (In modern terms, he was to perform nondestructive testing.)

Your group will be given one of six crowns. In our kingdom, aluminum is the most precious metal. At least one of the crowns is made of pure aluminum and at least one is a fake— not pure aluminum. You must design an experiment to determine if the crown you have is real or fake. You will have access to a sample of pure aluminum that you may use for comparison purposes if needed. You will need to do your own research for this experiment. The experiment you design is up to you, with the following constraints: (1) it must be safe, (2) we must have the equipment for it here at the school, (3) it must be nondestructive, and (4) it must be approved by Mr. M. (Note: Nondestructive means you cannot bend, cut, scratch, or change in any way the crown you are testing. Should you do so, the king will sentence you to the dungeon [translation: you will fail].)

The first thing you as a group must do is brainstorm at least four ways to determine if the crown is faked or not. You must do this without any help from computers, the Internet, or anyone else except members of your group. After you have come up with your ideas, you can then research them. During this part you may use computers and the Internet. Based on your research you must then decide on the method you will use to test your crown. All of your

---

brainstorming ideas must be written in your lab notebook and noted in your lab report in the background section. Then you must indicate your reasoning for why you chose the particular method that you did. This will be your first formal lab report that you will complete.

Your group must submit a typed, preliminary lab procedure to Mr. M. explaining the nondestructive experiment(s) that you plan to do. You can show it to me or e-mail it to me at my school address. It should include an explanation of the experiment, including step-by-step procedures and a good research design hypothesis (see STEM handbook Ch. 4 if you need more information). *The procedure must be approved by me before you begin.*

Your report must be typed and should follow the directions for writing a formal lab report in the chemistry shared folder. It will be graded using the Lab Report Rubric included in this document. Please read the article "Writing a Formal Lab Report" (hyperlinked for students) in your chemistry shared folder and follow the rubric closely. *This lab will be critiqued closely.*

After your procedure has been approved, you may begin. Please note that accuracy will be of vital importance. You will be measuring very small amounts, and any error you have will be drastic. A good experiment will also require repeated measurements.

### Student Lab Report

### Abstract

Crown A is pure aluminum because the density of Crown A is less than the density of pure aluminum, which is 2.7 g/mL. The results show that the higher the volume, the lower the density is.

### Introduction

The purpose of King's crown lab was to examine the density of the crowns and determine if they were pure aluminum inside. King Hiero suspected that the goldsmith filled the inside of the crown with the same weight of silver. The king hired Archimedes to determine if the wreath was pure gold. Archimedes' principle is that the weight of the water displaced is the same as the weight of the object. The volume of the crown was found using this principle. If crown A is near the density 2.7 g/mL, then the crown is pure aluminum.

### Materials and Methods

- bucket with a spout
- crown A
- 250 mL graduated cylinder
- pipette
- water
- balance
- 2 buckets

### Experimental Procedure

The first method used was filling a bucket inside a larger bucket until one drop spilled over the edge. Once the bucket looks filled to the top, start using a pipette until one drop goes over. This made sure that the bucket was completely filled to the top, and the results were a little more accurate. Find the mass of the crown before setting the crown in the water by putting it on a digital balance. Record results. Place the crown in the bucket once the water stops dripping. The water flowing into the larger bucket is the water displaced. When the

*(Continued)*

(Continued)

water stops dripping, carefully take the bucket filled with water out of the larger bucket. Pour the displaced water into the graduated cylinder and measure at the meniscus.

The second method was using the bucket with a spout. Fill the bucket up to the spout. When getting close to spilling the water, start using the pipette and carefully add water drop by drop. Keep adding water until one drop flows out. Measure the mass of the crown before lowering it into the water by placing it on a digital balance. Record results. Place the graduated cylinder directly beneath the spout, and set the crown into the water. The graduated cylinder needs to stay in place until the water completely stops dripping. Once the water is done, set the graduated cylinder on a level surface and read the measurement.

## Results

|         | Mass (g) | Volume (mL) | Density (g/mL) |                 |
|---------|----------|-------------|----------------|-----------------|
| Trial 1 | 65.63    | 50.1        | 1.31           |                 |
| Trial 2 | 68.79    | 80.0        | 1.16           |                 |
| Trial 3 | 69.21    | 45.0        | 1.54           |                 |
| Trial 4 | 69.88    | 52.2        | 1.34           | Average density |
|         |          |             |                | 1.34 g/mL       |

## Percentage of Error

|         | Accepted density (g/mL) | Estimated density (g/mL)      | Percentage of error |
|---------|-------------------------|-------------------------------|---------------------|
| Trial 1 | 2.7                     | 1.31                          | 51.5%               |
| Trial 2 | 2.7                     | 1.16                          | 57.0%               |
| Trial 3 | 2.7                     | 1.54                          | 43.0%               |
| Trial 4 | 2.7                     | 1.34                          | 50.4%               |
|         |                         | Average percentage of error   | 50.5%               |

The calculation for density is mass divided by volume. This calculation was performed for all 4 trials. The average density of Crown A was 1.34 g/mL. The percentage of error for the experiments can be found from accepted density minus the estimated density, and that answer divided by the accepted density. Multiply by 100 at the end for the percentage.

## Discussion

The expected results of the lab would have been a 2.7 g/mL density for every trial done in the experiment. The reason the results differed would have been different methods used. Allowing the water to spill over the side of a pan into another bucket, the results should be a little larger because the water dripping over the edge in the beginning of the experiment would not have been removed from the bucket. Another reason would be the equipment used. No scientific instruments were used except for the pipette. The buckets with the spout were created with a bucket with a hole drilled in the side and a piece of pipe hot glued into the hole.

**Conclusion**

From comparing the average density in the experiments and the accepted density value, it can be concluded that Crown A is indeed constructed of pure aluminum, even though the results can say that the average density of Crown A is 1.34 g/mL.

**References**

"Archimedes' Principle." *Archimedes' Principle*. N.p., n.d. Web. 29 Sept. 2014. Abbey Bueltel, Corey Fennel, Austin Fleener, Rachel Gangstad.

## Score and Explanation

This student work scores a 4 in *construction of knowledge* in science. According to the scoring criteria, "to score high, student's work must be original, and not merely a restatement of knowledge previously given in a text." Because each aspect of the lab requires original thinking, it would be easy to assume that the student work would score high; however, in order to verify our assumption we have to analyze each aspect of this lab to find evidence to support our score. In fact, there are several reasons to support that almost all of the student's lab report shows evidence of scientific interpretation, analysis, and evaluation.

First, we know that students do not know how many crowns are real or fake and could not rely on a process of elimination, waiting until one of the groups found the fake or real crown. Instead, each group had to work independently from other groups, designing experiments independently and determining the fake or real status of their group's crown. Therefore, we can conclude that this lab report is unique among submissions by other groups.

The second aspect of the student work that shows high *construction of knowledge* is the lab design. Each group is responsible for designing an experiment using items that can be found in class after brainstorming at least four possible designs. We do not see the brainstorming portion of the group's discussion and therefore can't use this as evidence in our score; however, because the teacher has pre-approved all the experiments, we can assume that students did "decide among procedures" and selected the experiment described in this this lab. Another way in which students showed they were thinking like scientists when doing their procedures can be seen in the data tables in the Results section. These show they gathered data from multiple trials and calculated the percentage of error for each trial.

The next example of strong *construction of knowledge* is found in the Discussion section. In this section, the student interprets the data and offers an analysis of why the actual results and the expected results differ, including the limited scientific equipment used and the overall impact of using water spillage to measure density. Finally, the student concludes that Crown A is constructed of pure aluminum despite a discrepancy between the group's findings (1.34 g/mL) and the expected results of 2.7 g/mL.

In addition to the uniqueness of this lab report, each step of the lab provides evidence of scientific interpretation, analysis, synthesis, or evaluation via students' hypothesizing, describing patterns, making models or simulations, building scientific arguments, or deciding among or inventing procedures. Indeed, that almost all of the student's work shows scientific thinking supports the score of 4.

## Instruction—Standard 1: Higher Order Thinking

> *Standard Summary: Instruction involves students in manipulating information and ideas by synthesizing, generalizing, explaining, hypothesizing, or arriving at conclusions that produce new meaning and understandings for them.*

Higher order thinking (HOT) requires students to organize, interpret, analyze, synthesize, or evaluate information about themes, concepts, and problems in order to draw a conclusion. Scoring is not intended to recognize some of these operations as more valued than others. Students demonstrating any one of these intellectual operations are demonstrating HOT, because each is a departure from retrieving, reporting, or reproducing facts, definitions, rules, and procedures, which is often what is emphasized in classrooms. In helping students become constructors (not just recipients) of knowledge, instruction for HOT often includes an element of uncertainty because the teacher may not be able to predict what conclusions students will reach.

Lower order thinking (LOT) occurs when students only receive or recite facts, definitions, conventions, or use rules and algorithms repeatedly. As information receivers, students are given specified knowledge conveyed through a reading, worksheet, lecture, or other media. The essence of instruction is to transmit knowledge, to practice procedural routines, or to test students' acquisition and recall of knowledge in forms previously given in texts, lectures, or other messages. Activities that may appear to involve HOT, such as presenting a research project to the class, may actually be dominated by LOT if students only report information that they have retrieved, without having organized or analyzed the information.

### Higher Order Thinking Rubric for Instruction

| Score | Criteria |
|---|---|
| 5 | Almost all students, almost all of the time, are performing HOT. |
| 4 | There is at least one major activity that occupies a substantial portion of the lesson in which most students perform HOT. |
| 3 | Most students are engaged in LOT for much of the lesson, but there is at least one significant question or activity in which many students perform some HOT. |
| 2 | Most students are engaged in LOT for most of the lesson, but at some point, at least some students perform HOT as a minor diversion within the lesson. |
| 1 | Most students are engaged only in LOT (i.e., they receive, recite, or participate in routine practice) and in no activities during the lesson do students go beyond LOT. |

## Example of Instruction: Third-Grade Science

In a third-grade science class, Ms. Ponder began a unit on rocks and minerals by showing students a wide range of materials, including cotton balls, Dixie cups, tin foil, paper plates, foam paper, and pipe cleaners. The teacher explained, "The Ponder Corporation is looking for scientists to engineer a structure that will be waterproof during heavy rain, strong enough to stay standing during high winds, and warm enough that people or animals do not get frostbite." Using provided materials, students worked with a partner to build a structure intended to meet these criteria. Students collected data on the properties of the provided materials by making predictions and testing each material. The results of these tests helped each pair select materials to design and build their structure.

Students spent time with their partners making in-depth predictions about the properties of each material.

- One pair discussed which items were waterproof. It was clear to them that the plastic Dixie cup was because it was holding the water. Other materials such as the marshmallow and the paper plate might seem waterproof at first, but may not be over time; for example, if you left food on it overnight, the plate would get soggy.

- Another student unrolled her cotton ball and explained to her partner that it must be warm because it looked just like the insulation her father had used when he remodeled their basement. These students each recorded that the main property of the cotton ball was its warmth (see Figure 2.5 on next page).

The next stage of the experiment was testing their predictions. Each pair had a water dropper, and hair dryers were located in different parts of the classroom for students to test a material for being windproof. Students discussed their predictions, tested the material, recorded the results, and described the properties of each material. Based on their results, the pairs then determined which materials they would select for their structures and how each could help them create a structure that withstands rain, wind, and cold.

Since this was an introductory lesson, pairs finished the lesson at different stages. Some pairs were still using their data to select their materials; a few drew diagrams based on the materials they selected, and many students moved into the building phase (see Figure 2.6 on next page).

The teacher noted many pairs seemed to be ignoring their data in favor of design, so she stopped the class and redirected them back to the main task, which depended on them making sure their structure would withstand cold temperatures when she put it outside with a thermometer inside, blew on it with a hair dryer, and poured water over

## Figure 2.5  Student Data Collection Table

| Material | Predicted Properties (strong, waterproof, flexible, transparent, layered, hard, soft, solid, etc.) | Use Yes or No, if yes for what? | Tested Properti |
|---|---|---|---|
| cotton ball | like inslation soft | yes | |
| craft stick | hard strong | yes | |
| straw | easy to bend hollow | not no sure | |
| toilet paper roll | cold thin not strong | not sure | |
| aluminum foil | strong | yes | |

## Figure 2.6  Students Comparing Their Sketch to Their Built Structure

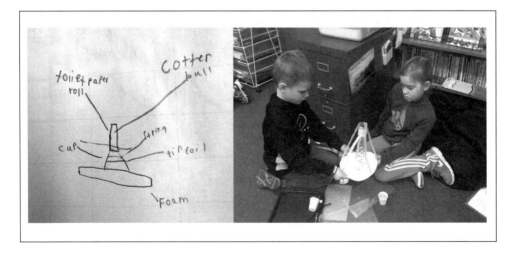

it to simulate rain. At this point, almost all of the pairs revisited their data and discussed making adjustments to their structures based on their data.

## Score and Explanation

This lesson scores 5 on HOT because almost all of the students spent nearly the entire lesson generating predictions and explanations about the properties of the building materials and testing them using a scientific method that included predictions, repeated tests, and recording the data collected. The variation in discussions among pairs indicated that even though the teacher required the same procedures for all, the data and conclusions were original and unique to each pair. Not only did students consider their prior experiences (e.g., when one student remarked about how similar the cotton ball looked to her father's insulation), but also they considered that knowledge when they made their predictions and tested their hypotheses, generating new knowledge, which led to a variety of structures that had differing construction rationales based on the analysis of each pair. The lesson illustrates that primary grade students can participate in a sustained activity in which they engage in original, higher order thinking throughout.

## CONCLUSION

This chapter concentrated on four artifacts that scored high on the standards and rubrics for *construction of knowledge*—tasks in math and Spanish, student work from high school chemistry, and an instructional segment in elementary science.

In Authentic Intellectual Work, successful *construction of knowledge* is best learned through a variety of experiences that call for this kind of cognitive work, not by explicitly teaching a set of discrete "thinking skills," divorced from the problems' contexts. Teachers often think of these operations as higher order thinking skills. Such *construction of knowledge* involves organizing, interpreting, evaluating, or synthesizing prior knowledge to solve distinct or novel problems. The examples in this chapter illustrate how students of all ages construct their own knowledge when the problems asked of them cannot be solved by routine use of information or skills previously learned.

# Chapter 3
## Disciplined Inquiry

## OVERVIEW

Constructing knowledge is critical to Authentic Intellectual Work (AIW), but it is insufficient. In addition, *construction of knowledge* should be grounded in what we call *disciplined inquiry.* As we described in Chapter 1, students engage in *disciplined inquiry* through three kinds of activities:

- Using a prior *knowledge base* often grounded in an academic or applied discipline. Students must have a solid knowledge base of facts, vocabularies, concepts, theories, algorithms, and other skills and processes necessary to conduct rigorous inquiry.

- Striving for *in-depth understanding* rather than superficial awareness. A knowledge base and relevant skills should be put to use to gain complex understanding of specific concepts and problems appropriate for a grade level. Such understanding develops as one uses methods and processes to investigate, imagine, propose, and test relationships among key facts, events, concepts, rules, and claims in order to clarify a specific problem or issue. Established procedures in a specific discipline can support inquiry. Students develop more complex understanding by drawing conclusions or generalizations and then explaining, justifying, or defending them.

- Developing and expressing understanding through *elaborated communication.* Students use complex forms of communication to conduct their work and to present and defend results. The tools they use—verbal, written, symbolic, graphic, and visual—provide qualifications, nuances, elaborations, details, and analogies woven into extended narratives, explanations, justifications, and dialogue that support their generalizations or conclusions.

*Disciplined inquiry* focuses on important concepts or themes in a subject area (e.g., symmetry, perspective, symbolism, democracy, evolution) or on compelling problems that may be either subject-specific or interdisciplinary (e.g., determining causes of deteriorating local water quality and proposing solutions). Concept or problem-based instruction is essential for *disciplined inquiry,* and many teachers must enhance their learning of what that is. A common confusion for some AIW teachers is the difference between concepts and facts or topics (for helpful clarification on concept-based instruction, see Erickson, 2002). While the AIW framework does not specify curriculum content, the content that teachers teach must be concept-, theme-, or problem-based for students to engage in *disciplined inquiry*.

In different subjects and grade levels, teachers often focus on disciplinary skills, methods, and processes as well as the conceptual content of a discipline. Drawing inferences in reading comprehension and applying the scientific method are two common examples. In our view, a skill or process can, when treated as a key idea in a discipline, be an indicator of *disciplined inquiry*. For example, a reading teacher may teach students how to draw an inference from text through exercises that build student understanding of *how* to use the skill to more accurately interpret written text. Students (as future voters) might try to discern important nuances between candidates' written policy statements when their general positions on issues seem identical. Students might then evaluate their own and peers' ability to successfully defend inferences they made from the texts. This teacher promotes *disciplined inquiry* more vigorously than one who teaches the skill only through exercises devoid of contexts that show *why* the skill is important and how it is used effectively.

To score high on the elaborated communication standard for *disciplined inquiry*, teacher tasks must demand a conclusion and explanation about the concepts, themes, or problems. For student work to score high, there must be evidence of conceptual understanding and elaborated communication of important concepts, themes, or problems. In the art task discussed later in this chapter, the artistic elements that students addressed could be considered either processes or concepts in the discipline. Many processes, like drawing inferences, evaluating evidence and argument, or graphing data, are generic and applicable to many subject areas. For scoring purposes, we usually see no need to distinguish between processes and concepts. Correct inference alone can't show understanding of a skill or process. Only some reasonably correct execution and elaboration of the skill or process can show understanding of it. A correct inference, however, might show understanding of a concept, depending how the problem is posed. The important consideration is the extent to which teacher tasks and instruction, and student work, put relevant knowledge to work for complex understanding of important content that is expressed through elaborated forms of communication, all at the appropriate grade level.

## EXEMPLARS FROM THE FIELD

This chapter presents artifacts of student work, teachers' tasks, and instruction in various subjects in high school, middle school, and elementary school. We show how standards for *disciplined inquiry* in student work—elaborated communication and conceptual understanding—can be stimulated by teaching standards for *disciplined inquiry* in teachers' tasks and instruction (namely, elaborated communication, deep knowledge, and substantive conversation). We start with a sample of elaborated communication in student work.

## Student Work—Standard 3: Elaborated Communication in Social Studies

*Standard Summary: The student provides an elaborated account of social studies ideas, concepts, theories, and principles through extended writing, talk, or another medium of communication.*

To score high, the student should provide (1) a conclusion, generalization, or argument and (2) support for it, in the form of examples, illustrations, details, or reasons. In addition, (3) the conclusion should be coherently linked to the support. Elaboration is coherent when the examples, illustrations, details, or reasons provide appropriate, consistent, and logical support for the conclusions, generalizations, or arguments. The score should be based not on the proportion of student work that contains conclusions and support but on the quality of elaborated communication, wherever it may be in the work.

### Student Work Rubric for Elaborated Communication in Social Studies

| Score | Criteria |
|-------|----------|
| 4 | Elaborated communication is exemplary. Explanations or arguments are clear, complete, accurate, coherent, and convincing, with no significant errors. |
| 3 | Elaboration is offered. Explanations or arguments are reasonably clear and accurate but lack sufficient support or coherence to be convincing. |
| 2 | Some elaboration is present, but explanations or arguments are significantly incomplete, contain significant errors, or are incoherent. |
| 1 | Little or no elaboration is offered. |

### Example of Student Work: High School Social Studies

The following example is an assignment from Ms. Johnson's interdisciplinary, multi-grade high school American Heritage course. The student's work responds to one part of a multi-part assignment in the Civic Ideals and American Heritage unit, which is focused on the question: How do our civic ideals influence our choices as leaders and citizens? The teacher, Ms. Johnson, informed the students that during the month of October, they would be using the 2012 presidential election as a way to investigate the status of our civic ideals today. The assignment and a sample of corresponding student work are shown in Figure 3.1.

**Figure 3.1  Letter to a 2012 Voter**

---

### Assignment

We have spent the first few weeks of the course learning about the foundations of American society. Our early founders worked diligently to create a nation and a government that would endure for generations. Early documents, including the Declaration of Independence, the Constitution, and the Bill of Rights, attempted to establish the civic ideals that would make our nation last. In the 1830s and 1840s, the Transcendentalists felt Americans had lost their way, and they wrote extensively about the ideals that might redirect the national conscience to the very foundations of liberty, equality, and individuality.

**Assignment:** Write a 600- to 800-word letter to a registered voter of your choice, and explain why you encourage that person to vote for a particular candidate. Your letter should provide developed responses to the following questions:

- What are the civic ideals embraced by your chosen candidate?
- What do the civic ideals of your candidate reveal about the kind of leader he might be?
- How do those ideals compare to the enduring civic ideals embraced by the founding fathers and the Transcendentalists?
- How do our civic ideals affect your reasons for supporting this particular candidate?
- Are there any civic ideals your candidate does not embrace? If so, why are these less important than the ones you have identified?
- Your supporting details must include the required specific support:
  - three specific passages from class readings to show evidence of the civic ideals of early America (include source title and page number using in-text citation)
  - specific examples from your candidate field research
  - unpacking of examples to show how they support your conclusions

### Student Work Sample From High School American Heritage Class

Dear Mr. Undecided,

Presidential elections are coming up in a few days. It is not too late to decide who you will vote for. There are many choices but in reality only two people can win. The winner will have to be President Obama or Governor Romney. The parties do not matter because in the end it all is down to who can save this country. The best choice for president is Obama.

Being the head of a middle class family, Obama is the candidate that will be most helpful to you. He has an amazing plan to rebuild this once great nation. His plan includes education, jobs, American energy, government spending cuts, and to end America's wars. Education is important to any nation's prosperity and success.

Benjamin Franklin even said "Genius without education is like silver in the mine" (Poor Richard's Almanac). Obama's plan will set a national standard for education. Better training for teachers and smaller class sizes makes it easier for children to learn and prosper. To help the next generations, training will also be put into place for jobs being brought to America. Crevecoeur once said, while America was young, in *Letters from an American Farmer*, "whose

*(Continued)*

(Continued)

Labors and prosperity will one day cause great changes in the world" (4). For Crevecoeur's dream to happen we need jobs. Obama is encouraging large companies to invest in America through tax cuts and other benefits. Four and a half million manufacturing jobs are being brought to the United States through Obama's plan. Small businesses will be supported through tax cuts and the car industry, revived. Jobs will also go to supporting the country in self-reliant energy. Using sources from America will also boost the economy since less will be bought from the Middle East. This is part of cutting spending to regain ground in the economic world. In fixing the home before worrying about the rest of the world Obama decided to bring our troops home. All of this helps people and families live independently, which the Transcendentalists believed in.

Obama is supporting women's rights and equality with men. His plans create more equal hiring between genders. Pay will be equal between men and women of the same ranking. Obama fought to keep funding for Planned Parenthood. He is working on making screenings for breast cancer and other issues more available and affordable. Obama believes women have the right to choose over their own body.

Recently North East America has been devastated by Super Storm Sandy. Obama, with the common good in mind, left his campaign trail to help the crippled region. This shows his true caring and sympathy for the United States and her people. He put a lot of effort into it and was even told, he did a good job by Chris Christie, a Republican. The leader of the Transcendentalists, Emerson, once said in "Self Reliance," "A man is relieved and gay when he has put his heart into his work and done his best" (2). Transcendentalists play a major role in the morals of our society and improvements on our government. Obama definitely showed true care and put his heart into his work. It is the President's job to be there when the people need him. He did and is doing all he can to help the entire area.

Obama is trying to get re-elected as everyone knows. He has helped this country with unemployment going down, now below eight percent. Obama brought justice to Bin-Laden by taking him out, which also helps protect the United States. The killing of the U.S. representative in Libya caused Obama to increase security for our other ambassadors so that our citizens abroad are safe. The removal of troops in Afghanistan is good because it is a war that can never be won without killing innocent civilians and it was an unnecessary expense.

I highly encourage voting for Obama as president. His second term will bring great benefits and change to everyone around the world. Even if this letter has been unable to help you decide which candidate to vote for look into Obama's plan at www.barackobama.com.

Sincerely, NG

## Score and Explanation

The student work scores 4 on elaborated written communication because throughout the work, the student stated specific support and evidence for concerns of the undecided voter. Generalizations and conclusions about how President Obama will help this country are coherently presented, and the support offered includes specific examples from current events or historical references. Though some teachers wanted to score it lower because the student failed to connect the arguments to the assignment's focus on leadership and civic ideals, meeting the demands of an assignment is not required to score high on *elaborated communication*. Our rubric requires only logical and coherent support that is coherently linked to a generalization, appropriate for the grade level and discipline. Later in the chapter we discuss evidence of student conceptual understanding for instruction.

## Teacher Task—Standard 2: Elaborated Communication in Another Subject

*Standard Summary: The task asks students to express a conclusion or conclusions about concepts, themes, theories, observations, procedures, or problems and to support their conclusions through coherent explanation or reasoning that involves elaborated use of language (written, oral, or other forms of visual/auditory expression), rather than brief declarations.*

### Teacher Task Rubric for Elaborated Communication in Any Subject

| Score | Criteria |
|---|---|
| 3 | Full elaboration: The task asks students to express conclusions about concepts, themes, theories, observations, procedures, or problems *and* to support their conclusions through coherent explanation or reasoning that involves elaborated use of language, rather than brief declarations. |

### Example of a Task: Eighth-Grade Art

Mr. Thompson assigned students to create their own drawings consistent with the style of M. C. Escher, and to evaluate how their drawing did or did not effectively use certain artistic elements. Students began by sketching their hands and drawing details such as knuckles and fingernails. The hands were shaded with different values to create realism. The students' final piece included drawing their hand holding a pencil as in Figure 3.2. After completing the drawing, students were given the task shown in Figure 3.3.

**Figure 3.2  Drawing**

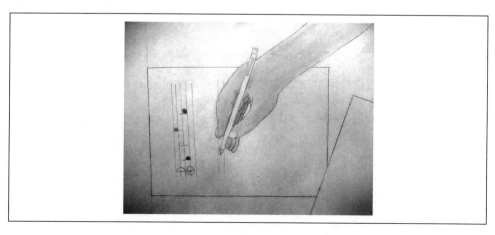

**Figure 3.3   Writing Task in Art**

**Writing Reflection**

Now that you are finished with your Escher-inspired hand drawing, your role changes from that of artist to art critic. Take a closer look at your drawing by analyzing it using the following vocabulary words. Be specific in your use of language, and support your thoughts by explaining how you've used each of the elements in your drawing. Remember to be specific and avoid statements such as this: "I like it because it has nice contours"; instead, try to explain how you used contours, proportion, values, texture, and space to create your artwork. Use the bottom of the page to judge your artwork. Once you've decided whether your artwork has success or lacks success, justify that decision by describing what it is that made your artwork successful, or describe areas that you may need to work on for future drawings.

**Contour Line**

_____

_____

**Value/Tonal Range**

_____

_____

**Proportion**

_____

_____

**Texture**

_____

_____

**Space**

_____

_____

ARTWORK HAS SUCCESS or LACKS SUCCESS

**Things I did right:**

_____

_____

---

**Things I might try differently:**

_____

_____

_____

---

*Score and Explanation*

This task scores 3 on elaborated communication because after creating an original drawing following a famous artist, students make overall judgments about the success of their drawings and use key artistic terms (*contours, proportion, values, texture,* and *space*) to critique them. Thus, the task asks for full elaboration (conclusion and support) that explains how they used artistic elements in their drawings. Through this elaboration, the teacher's expectations reflected in the task required students to show their understanding of important artistic elements (concepts). Conceivably, students could produce high-quality illustrations (*construction of knowledge* through a creative piece of art) but still may or may not have a solid understanding of the relevant artistic elements. A high-scoring task explicitly expects students to elaborate on that understanding.

We note that the assignment in the American Heritage class also scores a 3 for this standard of teacher tasks. In a similar fashion to the art task, the "Letter to a 2012 Voter" assignment asks students to make conclusions and support them in order to show their understanding of civic ideals.

## Teacher Task—Standard 2: Elaborated Communication in Mathematics

*Standard Summary: The task asks students to express a solution to or conclusions about mathematical concepts, theorems, procedures, or problems and to support their conclusions through coherent explanation or reasoning that involves elaborated use of language (written, oral, or other forms of visual/auditory expression), rather than brief statements.*

### Teacher Task Rubric for Elaborated Communication in Mathematics

| Score | Criteria |
|---|---|
| 3 | Full elaboration: The task asks students to express conclusions about mathematical concepts, theorems, procedures, or problems *and* to support their conclusions through coherent explanation or reasoning that involves elaborated use of language and/or diagrams/equations, rather than brief statements. |

In our work with teachers, we hear a concern from some primary teachers that their students can't be expected to understand important concepts in much depth or communicate in complex or elaborated ways. While we certainly recognize the importance of developmentally appropriate expectations, younger students can in fact be held to more rigorous cognitive demands. Consider this math task from a first-grade classroom.

## Example of a Task: First-Grade Math

On a whiteboard, Ms. Wax shows her students examples of different geometrical shapes, grouped according to symmetrical and nonsymmetrical shapes. She explains and defines symmetry and nonsymmetry. Then she poses this assignment:

- On your own whiteboards, draw your own shapes and divide them into two groups: shapes that are symmetrical and shapes that are nonsymmetrical.

- Pick two shapes that are symmetrical. Explain why they are symmetrical, not just by saying they are the same shape but by telling what specific parts of the shapes are the same.

- Pick two shapes that are not symmetrical. Explain why they are not symmetrical, not just by saying they are different but by telling what specific parts of the shapes are different.

### Score and Explanation

This task scores 3 on elaborated communication since it requires students to state conclusions (e.g., "these shapes are symmetrical") and support those conclusions. Students show their understanding of this math concept by illustrating and verbally explaining, both of which are appropriate communication forms for primary students, whose writing skills might limit the expression of their mathematical understanding. As students progress through the grades, their level of understanding is extended as they tackle different kinds of symmetry (e.g., rotational symmetry). The important point is that from the early grades, learning expectations include grade level–appropriate elaborated forms of communication, through which students demonstrate some conceptual understanding.

## Instruction—Standard 2: Deep Knowledge and Student Understanding

*Standard Summary: Knowledge is deep when it focuses on a concept, theme, or problem central to an academic, professional, or applied discipline. . . . For students, knowledge is deep when they develop complex understandings of these central concepts. Students can demonstrate systematic, integrated, or holistic understanding when they successfully discover relationships, solve problems, construct explanations, and/or draw conclusions that represent "new" knowledge.*

**Instruction Rubric for Deep Knowledge and Student Understanding**

| Score | Criteria |
|-------|----------|
| 5 | Knowledge is very deep. The lesson sustains a focus on a significant disciplinary concept, theme, or problem *and* almost all students do at least one of the following: demonstrate understanding by arriving at a reasoned explanation or argument of how they answered a question related to a central concept, theme, or problem in a discipline, or demonstrate their understanding of the problematic nature of information and/or ideas central in the discipline. |

Because the example for instruction illustrates both Standard 2 (Deep Knowledge and Student Understanding) and Standard 3 (Substantive Conversation), it appears following descriptions of each standard.

## Instruction—Standard 3: Substantive Conversation

*Standard Summary: Classes with high levels of substantive conversation focus on the substance of subject matter and include considerable teacher-student and/or student-student interaction. Substantive conversation has three main features:*

1. *Talk is about concepts, themes, and problems in the discipline and includes higher order thinking such as making distinctions, applying ideas, forming generalizations, or raising questions, not just the reporting of experiences, facts, definitions, or procedures.*

2. *Conversation involves the sharing of ideas. Sharing is best illustrated when participants respond directly to previous speakers by explaining themselves or asking questions to clarify other speakers' statements. Conversation of this sort is not completely scripted or controlled by one party.*

3. *The dialogue builds on participants' statements to promote a coherent collective (rather than only individualized) understanding of a disciplinary concept, theme, or problem. This is illustrated in seminars or small-group discussions that, through sustained conversations, integrate the contributions of all participants into common understandings shared by the group. For our purposes, a sustained conversation is defined as at least three consecutive interchanges between persons in the class.*

**Instruction Rubric for Substantive Conversation**

| Score | Criteria |
|-------|----------|
| 5 | Almost all students participate in all three features of substantive conversation, and at least one example of sustained conversation occurs. |

### Example of Instruction: Ninth-Grade English Language Arts

Teachers nurture all three features of *disciplined inquiry* through their classroom instruction. We identify the extent of success in a particular lesson through the above two standards. Our example here is from a ninth-grade English language arts class. Students in Ms. O'Connor's class participated in a blog over multiple days to both advance and demonstrate their understanding of a central theme of the novel *The Help* by Kathryn Stockett. Ms. O'Connor explained,

> To prepare for learning beyond the classroom in our increasingly interconnected world, students must use digital tools to communicate and collaborate with the common goals of questioning, examining, and publishing their ideas. As we implement various methods, derived from the Common Core and AIW, we must first remember that students' learning is driven by authentic opportunities to research and reflect, manage problems, and make informed decisions. Technology is merely the evolving vehicle that allows us to aid students in this growth.

To scaffold students' learning and their use of challenging questions, the teacher uses the following question continuum for a number of different activities, including this one.

---

**Question Continuum**

Please remember we need questions of all numbers, 2 through 4, in order to comprehend. While it is important to ask type 2 questions, it should not be where are our questions are, otherwise we will have only a surface understanding of what we read, view, or hear.

4: Have to look between the lines and look and reread the question or reread the story; causes discussion that leads to multiple questions; may not have answer, requires thought; can be argued; piggy-back thought; leads to other thoughts; uses facts to create meaning

3: Makes you think more than one minute; causes discussion that leads to multiple answers; gets your mind going to more than one answer; causes discussion that leads to finding an answer; question could be thick or thin depending on how the reader reads it

2: Yes or no/thin or definite answer; one answer; question can be answered in a few words; reader can find the answer by looking it up; factual

1: Question doesn't relate

---

Figure 3.4 gives the teacher's directions to engage in an online discussion and transcript for one group that included five students. Normally when scoring instruction, the percentage of students in a class who participate influences the score. However, for our purposes here, we use the conversation among the five students in this group as a representative sample for the kind of conversation that occurred in all small groups. The discussion is in response to an archival photo that depicts separate drinking fountains for "Whites" and "Colored."

**Figure 3.4 English Language Arts Lesson Activity**

---

### Blog, *The Help*

Find an article or piece of art/image that relates to the theme of your novel. Write a response in which you give at least three specific examples of how it connects to your theme. Be sure to include and explain your textual evidence from your novel to support your comparison.

- Remember to use the rubric in the menu bar to guide your writing.
- Each student makes a minimum of five comments.

**Keep in mind while posting:**

- All your peers will see your comments.
- Be kind, yet push the conversation. You may agree with the blogger, but you must add some more evidence or a new idea.
- If you disagree with the blogger, be sure to state it kindly. For example, "I understand you may think that Huck is intelligent, but I think *street smarts* might be a better way to describe him."
- Provide evidence for your claim.
- Ask *thick* questions.

#### *The Help* by Kathryn Stockett

**Initial Post**

**Katherine.** March 28, 2014, 10:28 a.m. This image relates to the book because it shows segregation in 1962. In the book Miss Leefolt builds a separate bathroom for Aibileen because her friends don't want to use the same bathroom as the help. Miss Hilly said that "It's just plain dangerous. Everybody knows they carry different diseases than us." Once Miss Leefolt builds a bathroom outside for the help it isn't very nice. This picture shows that in the 1960s white people didn't think much of African Americans and they thought that they were better than them, which is how the white people think in the book. At the beginning of the book Aibileen and Minny are riding the bus and they can stay seated if a white person comes onto the bus thanks to Rosa Parks. This also connects because segregation is finally starting to stop, but things are still very segregated. All the white people in this book think they are better than the African Americans/the help.

**12 comments**

**Adam.** March 31, 2014, 10:05 a.m. I thought that the African-Americans had their own separate bus to ride on? Also this picture shows much symbolism as it shows what life was like back then and the way people were treated back then. My question is did the Americans back then never wanted to be equal? Or did they think they were too good for the African-Americans? Lastly I agree with you Katherine, that segregation is finally stopping. One example is that today we have an African-American president. Americans voted for him as president. Another thing is I felt like in the book, only women were the big and bad ones always standing up to the Americans just like Rosa Parks.

**Katherine.** April 6, 2014, 4:44 p.m. Adam—I don't think that the white people ever wanted to be equal with the African Americans since they treated them poorly. But some people, like Miss Skeeter, do treat the help the same as everyone else. Yes, segregation is stopping

*(Continued)*

---

(Continued)

now but there is still some racism today. I am not sure if there will ever be a day when people aren't still kind of racist.

**Valentina.** April 2, 2014, 6:50 a.m. I like your picture choice! It shows what Aibileen had to go through with Mrs. Leefolt having a new bathroom in the garage for her to use instead of using the same bathroom as the "white folk."

**Katherine**. April 6, 2014, 4:45 p.m. Thanks! :)

**Olivia.** April 2, 2014, 7:07 a.m. I like your choice for the photo, I think it fits very well. Do you think that the Help wanted to be segregated? It talks about the white ladies gossip and how they want segregation, but what do you think of the Help's opinion? I would think that they know it will never be quite as equal, but they don't really seem to want integration either. Do you think this has to do with a fear factor, or that maybe they just don't want anything to do with the whites? Aibileen doesn't seem to mind her new bathroom, I think maybe she just knows that it won't be better for a long time and is used to the way they are treated. Do you think that the women were the only ones standing up for integration? Or were the men part of it too? I think that maybe Rosa Parks is the person who inspired the women to help out with the issue. How do you think the story would have been different if ladies like Ms. Parks hadn't stood up yet? Would the maids have had enough courage to write the book? Or would they try to leave it to the men?

**Katherine**. April 6, 2014, 4:52 p.m. I don't think that the help wants to be segregated, it's just that they do not trust the white people. Minny said that Aibileen switches jobs when the babies start to think that African Americans are not as good as white people. So I don't think that the help wants to be segregated but the reason they aren't super supportive of integration is because they do not trust the white people and that is why the avoid white people and are cautious of what they say around them. Well I'm not sure if men and women played an equal role in integration but I do think that the story would have been different if people like Rosa Parks had not stood up for what they believe in. I don't think that Aibileen would have helped write the book because she would have thought that there was no hope for changing things.

**Adam.** April 2, 2014, 8:51 a.m. I like this picture and I think it fits very good with the book and the point of time they are in and there is a quote on page 51, "I'll try," I say, even though I've never told a white woman what to do before I don't really know how to start. I think that connects to this a lot. Do you think its because her friends that she make her put a bathroom out there?

**Desirae.** April 3, 2014, 9:18 a.m. I agree with what you're saying Katherine but I suggest next time don't pick such an obvious picture. When I saw the picture I could of guessed what you were going to say without even reading what you had said. What do you mean by segregation is stopping? Do you mean then or now? If you are refereeing to now I somewhat agree with you. I honestly don't think it will ever stop. I know people who aren't even allowed to date black people . . . isn't that just as bad? I agree with what Adam said about how it's changed a lot with having an African American president now. That's amazing knowing what all happened in the past. If you mean back then segregation was changing I disagree. They still got treated like diseases and they didn't get treated how white people got treated.

**Katherine.** April 6, 2014, 4:58 p.m. When I said segregation is stopping I was referring to back then in the 1960s. In the story segregation was only beginning to stop. People like Rosa Parks were some of the very first people to stand up for the rights that they should have. Even though they were still treated horribly you can tell that change is starting, even though it is very small so far. I completely agree with you that the world will probably always be kind of segregated and never truly equal. It's especially sad that even nowadays that there is still some segregation since we have an African American president.

**Desirae.** April 8, 2014, 8:44 a.m. But segregation wasn't stopping back then . . . it was always around. Like for example in the book when Mrs. Leefolt wanted to build a separate bathroom for Aibileen. How is it stopping? If you think it is stopping what specific ideas do you have from the book that shows segregation is stopping?

**Adam.** April 7, 2014, 10:06 a.m. Katherine—Yes there is still some racism going on throughout the world today, I was just trying to say it's partially fading. Also Katherine why do you think Ms. Skeeter is treating the African-Americans like that? . . . because in the book she is so nice and generous to them.

**Desirae.** April 8, 2014, 8:53 a.m. Adam, I agree with you. I feel like it will always be hovered over us though. No matter if you are white or black, there's always going to be that guiltiness. I think Ms. Skeeter is treating the blacks just like any other person is because she was so close to Constantine so she feels like she owes it to all of them. Well not necessarily "owe" any thing to the help but she just wants to be there for them because she has a burden on her heart that she made Constantine leave. I know it wasn't her fault but she will always have that feeling on her heart, and she's not gonna stop until something changes.

### Scores and Explanation

This lesson activity scores 5 for deep knowledge and student understanding. Through a blog format, the students conducted a discussion connecting a major theme of the novel to a photograph chosen by one of them. All students in the class (a) started a blog discussion by identifying an artifact connected to themes of *The Help*, (b) responded to peers' initial contributions, and (c) responded to peers' responses to their own contributions. Some aspect of the overarching concept of inequality was explored in their online discussions. The rubrics require that "almost all students" demonstrate understanding by arriving at a reasoned explanation or argument; this example shows only one group, but other groups did similar work.

During the entire online discussion, students sustained a focus on the theme of segregation and connected the theme to their text, *The Help*. Students asked each other questions and made connections to the present day, thereby extending their understanding. For example, Olivia raised the possibility that African Americans in the novel might not have wanted integration. Desirae challenged Katherine on her choice of the photo and pressed her for further explanation of segregation, past and present. At the same time, Adam's word choice suggests there is certainly room for further understanding; variation in student conceptual understanding is not unexpected in any lesson, and the standards for instruction ask for a global judgment. In this regard, a high score for any standard on any artifact does not mean it cannot be improved upon. But overall, the students here both demonstrated and expanded their understanding by arriving at reasoned explanations of how they answered a question related to a central theme.

This lesson activity also scores a 5 for substantive conversation. The students' discussion exhibited the three required features of substantive conversation: contributions *focused on a theme* of the novel with higher order thinking; exchanges entailed *sharing of ideas* not dominated by any one student or a predetermined idea established by the teacher; and the dialogue *built to promote collective understanding* of the theme. The conversation was sustained through more than three interchanges that were substantively linked on segregation. Almost all students in the class participated fully in similar online discussions, which is required for the highest score.

The high scores for both standards do not mean that student understanding of important themes related to the novel is complete or could not be developed further. In fact, Ms. O'Connor had students follow up their blog posts with oral discussions in small groups during subsequent class periods. Then, as a culminating task, students wrote concluding short essays in which the teacher expected further analysis and elaboration of students' self-evaluations ("How have you grown with providing textual evidence to support your thoughts?") and their understanding of the literary theme of inequality.

Rudyanto Wijaya/iStock/Thinkstock

## CONCLUSION

This chapter concentrated on four artifacts that scored high on the standards and rubrics for *disciplined inquiry*—a student essay in social studies, teacher tasks in art and math, and an instructional segment in English language arts.

Our conception of Authentic Intellectual Work requires students to (1) use a prior *knowledge base*, (2) strive for *in-depth understanding* rather than superficial awareness of central themes and concepts, and (3) develop and express their understanding through *elaborated communication*. We use the term *disciplined inquiry* to capture these three important dimensions of high-quality teaching and learning. The AIW standards and rubrics for disciplined inquiry help teachers design tasks and lessons, and evaluate student work, to enhance students' conceptual understanding and their ability to communicate that understanding to others.

# Chapter 4
## Value Beyond School

**OVERVIEW**

Efforts to reform schools often try to make learning more "relevant" to students, which frequently means including topics and activities that students enjoy, choose, or show enough interest in to participate with enthusiasm and little resistance. While relevance in this sense may engage students, it alone offers no assurance that students are involved in rigorous intellectual work. According to the Authentic Intellectual Work (AIW) framework, the best sense of relevance comes from not simply catering to students' interests or enjoyment, but making intellectual demands that provoke students to connect academic and conceptual learning to questions, problems, and issues that students face or are likely to face outside of school. Students' intellectual work in completing learning tasks that score high on such criteria have meaning to them beyond simply complying with demands of school. Examples of high-scoring student work are not included in this chapter because whether students perceive their work as having value beyond success in school or whether it actually has influence on an audience beyond school is not usually a key learning objective to be assessed. In contrast, a lesson or completed task can be scored on the extent to which it requires students to apply their knowledge to influence an audience beyond school. This criterion is often accepted as an important teaching objective.

**EXEMPLARS FROM THE FIELD**

In this chapter, we include examples of instruction and tasks from elementary and secondary school that illustrate how students apply academic knowledge to real-world issues or problems. The first examples are teacher tasks, one a high school math task and the other a fourth-grade music task. We also include an example of instruction in a fourth-grade integrated science and language arts class.

### Task—Standard 3: Value Beyond School in Mathematics

*Standard Summary: The task asks students to use a mathematics concept, theory, law, procedure, or problem to clarify, understand, or resolve situations in the world beyond school.*

Consider the extent to which students are asked to apply mathematical concepts, theorems, procedures, or problems to clarify, understand, or resolve situations, not whether the content or problem posed seems relevant to student interests. While relevance can increase student engagement, relevance alone doesn't necessarily require student understanding of how mathematics knowledge applies to situations and problems in the real world.

## Task Rubric for Value Beyond School in Mathematics

| Score | Criteria |
|---|---|
| 4 | The question, issue, or problem posed by the task requires students to apply mathematical concepts, theorems, procedures, or problems to clarify, understand, or resolve situations in the world beyond school. The kind of application requested helps students understand the utility of mathematics in the real world. Students must display, exhibit, or demonstrate their work in ways that will influence an audience beyond school, for example, by communicating what they have learned to others, advocating solutions to problems, providing assistance to people, creating products, or conducting performances. |
| 3 | The question, issue, or problem posed by the task requires students to apply mathematical concepts, theorems, procedures, or problems to clarify, understand, or resolve situations in the world beyond school. The kind of application requested helps students understand the utility of mathematics in the real world. However, there is no effort to influence an audience beyond school. |
| 2 | The question, issue, or problem posed by the task requires students to apply mathematical concepts, theorems, procedures, or problems to clarify, understand, or resolve situations in the world beyond school, but the kind of application requested is not likely to help students understand the utility of mathematics in the real world. |
| 1 | The task makes little or no demand for students to apply mathematical concepts, theorems, procedures, or problems to clarify, understand, or resolve situations in the world beyond school. |

## Example 1 of a Task: High School Mathematics

Mr. Deal gave the following task to students in several sections of his pre-calculus class. He told them that each section would be a company competing against other companies (sections), as described in Figure 4.1.

The assignment spanned 4 days and required each section of the class to work independently so as not to share information with a competitor. Each section could draw on mathematical knowledge from the teacher or other sources. But using the teacher as a consultant cost the sections points they would have to pay with whatever points they earned from completing the project.

### Score and Explanation

This task scores 3 on value beyond school because the problem of developing a computer program posed in the task requires students to translate the job of reupholstering a lampshade into mathematical equations that can be programmed for computer calculation of the shape and size of fabric. This demands they apply previously acquired

**Figure 4.1  Lampshade Company Competition**

You are an employee for the company LampshadesRUs, and the recent economic times caused a downturn in the company's business. There have been rumors of layoffs, and you and your team have been asked to brainstorm ideas that will create increased revenue for the company.

- During your brainstorming session you decide that there is a higher probability that customers will spend $5 on fabric to reupholster their old lampshades instead of purchasing a brand-new lampshade for $20.
- To save money on operation costs, your boss decides that this promotion will be largely automated. Customers will be able to submit orders online, and they will be asked to submit the following three facts: (1) radius of the top opening = ___ centimeters, (2) radius of the bottom opening = ___ centimeters, and (3) height of lampshade = ___ centimeters.
- After submitting the information, customers will be able to choose the design of their new fabric as well.  All the information will then be processed by a computer, which will determine the correct dimensions for the new swatch of fabric to be cut. However, for this to occur, the computers must be programmed with the correct equation that will be used to determine the shape and size of the fabric.
- Your assignment is to write that computer program.

The classmates in your class are now your colleagues in your company. Know that we have four companies competing against each other. Whichever company solves the problem first and successfully writes the program, runs it with customer specs, cuts out the fabric, and recovers an old lampshade will receive a bonus of 100 extra credit points. Larger classes may separate into teams, but you are still in the same company.

mathematical knowledge to a new and distinct real-world design and manufacturing problem. Students must apply and algebraically manipulate basic geometric formulas that deal with the Pythagorean theorem, circumference, segment lengths, ratios, and arc lengths. They must then compose a universal formula from the multiple geometric equations allowing them to compute the dimensions of a cover for any size lampshade given specific inputs. Based on these findings, they then write a calculator program that takes values submitted by the customers as inputs and calculate the desired measurements to cut the fabric correctly.

Having to pay a fee for outside consulting and the opportunity to receive a bonus for the team that solves the problem first further simulates real-world conditions of minimizing costs in a competitive economy and strengthens student understanding of the utility of mathematical knowledge beyond school. The task does not score 4 because it fails to require students to use their knowledge to influence an audience beyond school; the results of their mathematical problem solving are shared only within the high school mathematics class.

### Example 2 of a Task: Fourth-Grade Music

Ms. Boyd teaches elementary school music. After students have acquired a strong foundation in basic musical concepts, she gives them the opportunity to become composers. The teacher's purpose is to deepen student understanding of how musical concepts are utilized in composing, critiquing, and performing an original piece of music. Through this assignment, shown in Figure 4.2, students experience the role of a composer from the beginning of the creative process through the performance of their compositions. Students utilize the musical methods and processes that allow them to experience a composer's craft. All students in the fourth-grade music class apply knowledge in the musical discipline to create a new product. Each student composer presents his or her musical composition to an audience made up of peers and music boosters; a few go on to perform their pieces during the spring program.

**Figure 4.2  Lesson on Composing Music**

You have been commissioned by the music boosters to write a recorder composition for the annual fourth-grade spring program. The boosters and your classmates will vote on the top five compositions in fourth grade based on accuracy in notation, melodic complexity, and rhythm.

- You are encouraged to include all of the pitches we have learned in class (B, A, G, C, and D).
- Be sure to accurately notate both pitch and rhythm on a music staff. Also, pay close attention to the time signature. Your composition must be at least eight measures long. You must name your composition. Be sure to practice your composition because you will perform it for your classmates and the music boosters, who will vote on the final five compositions to be performed at the April 7th concert.

"Lolipops and Gumdrops" is an example of student work that has 23 measures in 4/4 with a variety of rhythmic patterns and recorder articulation.

## Score and Explanation

The scoring rubric here, for a non-core subject assignment, is basically the same as the one shown for mathematics. This task scores 4 on value beyond school. The problem posed—to create a composition for the recorder that meets specific criteria—requires students to apply musical concepts and procedures to the real-world challenge of creating a credible musical composition, that is, one that will garner approval from an actual audience. The task requires students to demonstrate their work to influence an audience beyond school because not only classmates but also the local community's musical boosters club will vote to select the final five best musical compositions.

# Instruction—Standard 4: Value Beyond School

*Standard Summary: Instruction involves students using knowledge or skills of an academic, professional, or applied discipline to study or work on a concept, theme, or problem in contexts beyond school.*

Authentic Intellectual Work employs knowledge, concepts, or processes used in academic, professional, or applied disciplines to understand situations and solve problems in contexts beyond school. Such issues and problems might relate to civic life, workplace experience, or personal affairs (e.g., experiences within the family, as a consumer, or during leisure time) that students have encountered or are likely to encounter in their lives outside school. When intellectual work in the classroom helps students address and understand situations and problems outside the classroom, we assume the work they do in class has value and meaning for them beyond the benefits of achieving success in school.

Intellectual work useful for answering questions, performing tasks, and solving problems posed only in the school context is less authentic because it serves only to certify students' level of competence or compliance with the norms and routines of formal schooling. Such work offers no assurance that students' knowledge or skills will have value and meaning in the world beyond school.

## Instruction Rubric for Value Beyond School

| Score | Description |
|---|---|
| 5 | Most students use knowledge or skills of an academic, professional, or applied discipline to study or work on a concept, theme, or problem in contexts beyond school. The students recognize the value of classroom knowledge/skills in understanding or addressing situations outside the classroom. They also apply their knowledge and skills to influence an audience beyond their classroom, for example, by communicating what they have learned to others, advocating solutions to social problems, providing assistance to people, creating products, or conducting performances that others will value. |
| 3 | Many students use knowledge or skills of an academic, professional, or applied discipline to study or work on a concept, theme, or problem in contexts beyond school. But only some of these students recognize the value of classroom knowledge/skills in understanding or addressing situations outside the classroom. |

*(Continued)*

(Continued)

| Score | Description |
|-------|-------------|
| 1 | There is no connection between the lesson and contexts beyond school. Knowledge or skills of an academic, professional, or applied discipline are not used to study or work on a concept, theme, or problem in contexts beyond school. The teacher may try to explain connections between academic learning and problems in nonschool contexts (e.g., the teacher might inform students that understanding Middle Eastern history is important for understanding the price of gasoline and oil in the United States), but students are not involved in applying such knowledge, nor do they recognize the value of classroom knowledge/skills in understanding or addressing situations outside the classroom. |

## Example of Instruction: Fourth-Grade English Language Arts and Science

Ms. Ryan and Ms. Wink collaborated on a interdisciplinary unit with their fourth graders. In the science part of this project students learned about three systems of the human body: skeletal system, muscular system, and central nervous system. The main idea was how the systems work together to cause movement, and students participated in a variety of experiments and activities to illustrate this.

After the unit was introduced in science class, students then researched the three body systems in more depth in language arts class. After being divided into three groups, each assigned to one body system, students learned how to organize their research findings into notes that helped them address three main essential questions:

- Why is this body system important?

- How does a person take care of this body system?

- What would happen if this body system broke down?

Three research centers were set up around the room with multiple nonfiction texts. While researching their topic, students read critically, trying to pick out the key details while also avoiding plagiarism by rewriting the information in their own words. They were instructed to organize notes according to their relevance to the main ideas.

Students had previously learned about the structure of paragraphs by using a graphic organizer resembling a hamburger. In it, the top bun is the topic sentence. The hamburger patty, cheese, lettuce, and tomatoes are the supporting details. The paragraph ends with a "killer conclusion," the bottom bun. During this unit, they applied that knowledge to compose a three-paragraph persuasive essay about the human body system they researched.

After writing the first draft, students revised and edited with peers and the teacher. After revising and editing, students typed the final draft as a Google document. The teacher gave feedback as comments on the electronic document. The final document was printed and showcased in a human body craft project, which is explained next.

Students applied their knowledge by creating a human body shape from construction paper, with shirt flaps that opened to reveal the typed essay. They decorated the clothing and hair on the body using scrapbook paper, yarn, buttons, and other materials donated by parents and friends.

When the projects were completed, the teacher sent a letter home to parents asking if those connected to health organizations in the community would volunteer to collect the projects and hang them up at these locations. The projects were distributed to a broad variety of medical locations and were showcased in area nursing homes, fitness centers, chiropractic offices, dentists' offices, hospitals, and doctors' offices.

As an extension to the human body project, students then collaborated to create life-sized human body posters (see Figure 4.3). In small groups, they began by tracing one student's body outline on butcher paper. The body shape was cut out and glued to a background poster. Using diagrams from nonfiction literature as references, students designed the parts of that body system on the poster. They labeled these parts using scientific vocabulary. The posters were displayed in prominent locations in the school to spur enthusiasm for such projects among the younger students in the building.

### Score and Explanation

Instruction for this project scores 5 for value beyond school. Most students used biology knowledge (of the human body's muscular, skeletal, or central nervous systems) and skills in language arts (paragraph structure, organizing notes and sources to address main ideas, steps in creating a persuasive essay) to diagram one body system and to

**Figure 4.3  Fourth Grader Working on Her Group's Human Body Poster[1]**

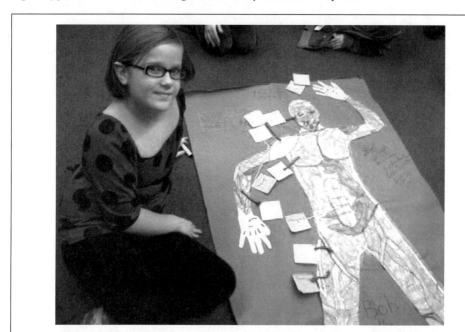

write to inform an audience about this topic. The students applied their knowledge and skills to influence audiences beyond their classroom by displaying their projects in health service–related businesses in the community and by displaying posters of their projects in school to influence younger students.

## CONCLUSION

In this chapter, we highlighted the third criterion for AIW, *value beyond school,* and showed how samples of teacher tasks and instruction can meet the relevant standard to a high degree. When many educators, and perhaps even non-educators, hear the term *authentic,* they typically assume this means *only* presenting students with problems relevant to students' personal interests or to a real-world situation. Our conception of Authentic Intellectual Work requires a lot more; namely, *construction of knowledge* using *disciplined inquiry* in academic or applied disciplines to address questions, issues, or problems that have meaning to students beyond simply completing assigned tasks in school and that produces work capable of influencing others.

# Afterword
## To Part II

The last three chapters have concentrated on artifacts of instruction, tasks, and student performance that score high on one of the three criteria for Authentic Intellectual Work. We close Part II with one final example, a high school science task that scores high on all three criteria: construction of knowledge, disciplined inquiry, and value beyond school. Any task or lesson that scores high on one or two of these criteria helps to promote Authentic Intellectual Work. However, when students experience learning opportunities that over time score high on all three criteria, their achievement will be higher, more equitably distributed, and include more Authentic Intellectual Work.

## Task—Standard 1: Construction of Knowledge in Science

*Standard Summary: The task asks students to organize, interpret, analyze, synthesize, or evaluate information in addressing scientific theories, laws, observations, concepts, procedures, or problems, rather than to retrieve or report information as previously given or to repeatedly apply previously learned procedures.*

| Score | Description |
|---|---|
| 3 | The task's dominant expectation is for students to organize, interpret, analyze, synthesize, or evaluate scientific information, rather than merely to reproduce information or to repeatedly apply previously learned procedures. |

## Task—Standard 2: Elaborated Scientific Communication

*Standard Summary: The task asks students to express a conclusion or conclusions about scientific theories, observations, concepts, procedures, or problems and to support their conclusions through coherent explanation or reasoning that involves elaborated use of language (written, oral, or other forms of visual/auditory expression), rather than brief declarations.*

| Score | Description |
|---|---|
| 3 | Full elaboration: The task asks students to express conclusions about a scientific theory, laws, observations, concepts, procedures, or problems *and* to support their conclusions through coherent explanation or reasoning that involves elaborated use of language and or diagrams/equations, rather than brief declarations. |

## Task—Standard 3: Value Beyond School in Science

*Standard Summary: The task asks students to use a scientific concept, theory, law, procedure, or problem to clarify, understand, or resolve scientific situations in the world beyond school.*

| Score | Description |
|---|---|
| 4 | The question, issue, or problem posed by the task requires students to apply scientific theories, laws, concepts, procedures, or problems to clarify, understand, or resolve situations in the world beyond school. The kind of application requested helps students understand the utility of science in the real world. Students must display, exhibit, or demonstrate their work in ways that will influence an audience beyond school, for example, by communicating to others what they have learned, advocating solutions to problems, providing assistance to people, creating products, or conducting performances. |

### Example of a Task: 10th-Grade Science

In a 10th-grade integrated science class, Dr. Stone presented her students with the following culminating task at the end of their unit of study on density. Her goal in this task was to have students evaluate the effectiveness of a measurement tool using scientific experimentation and the concept of density. Working in small groups, students had multiple days to complete the task.

Figure—The Booze Bulb Science Task

---

## Application Problem:  Does the Booze Bulb Really Work?

### Procedure

The science teacher from your school is the prom chaperone this year. To make sure that no one has "spiked" the punch at the dance, the teacher has created a new device called the "Booze Bulb" to test the drinks for "booze." You have been given one of the Booze Bulbs and your job is to determine if it actually works at detecting alcohol in drinks. Your group needs to provide scientific proof that it does or does not work. This will require that you experiment with a number of drinks with a variety of percentages of alcohol.  You may use isopropyl alcohol to simulate drinking alcohol.

WARNING:  DO NOT DRINK THIS SUBSTANCE!

Write down data from all of the experiments you try, and keep track of the procedure you follow during your experimenting. For example, here are some of the questions you will need to have data for: Does the bulb work with all types of drinks? What is the minimum amount of alcohol it will detect?  Record data as you go so that you are able to show all of your calculations and logic once your experimenting in completed.

### Summing Up

Answer *all* summing up questions on a separate sheet of paper, which also contains your data tables and calculations.

In light of the experiments you designed and carried out to provide scientific proof that the Booze Bulb works, write a technical report summarizing (1) your procedures, (2) your data, and (3) your conclusions. Be sure to include or refer the reader to a well-organized data table.

What science concept causes the Booze Bulb to have different results in different liquids? Explain how you think the bulb works **and explain the significance of the different colored balls.**

What applications, **other than testing drinks,** could **this device** have in the real world? **(Come up with at least two new uses.)**

Write a two-paragraph letter to your high school principal discussing the use of the Booze Bulb at prom.  Based on the results of your experiment, you may either praise the efforts of your science teacher for her innovative device used to help curb teenage drinking OR criticize the teacher for creating an instrument that has no scientific basis. **Be sure to provide the principal with directions on how to use the device.**

| Lab setup | easy | moderate | difficult |
|---|---|---|---|
| Calculations | easy | moderate | difficult |

*(Continued)*

(Continued)

| Reliability | excellent | good | fair |
|---|---|---|---|
| Interest | excellent | good | fair |
| Lab time | 1 class | 1 class | + 1 class |
| Process skills | Interpreting data | Experimenting | Observing |
| | Measuring | Predicting | Inferring |

## Booze Bulb Scoring Rubric

| Data | • All data is displayed in a data table |
|---|---|
| | • Table has correct headings with units |
| | • Data is neatly displayed |
| | • Data quantity and quality are sufficient to answer the question |
| **Procedure** | • Procedure explains how quantitative data was collected |
| | • Procedure is sound (including having a control and testing a variety of liquids) |
| | • Procedures include all steps |
| **Technical report (Sum Up #1)** | • Summarizes procedures |
| | • Summarizes findings and refers reader to data tables |
| | • Conclusion statement is correct based on data collected |
| **How it works (Sum Up #2)** | • Explains how the Booze Bulb works and includes the concept of density |
| | • Includes explanation of why the balls behave differently |
| **Real-world applications (Sum Up #3)** | • Applications listed are related to the density of liquids |
| | • At least two applications are listed that differ from the drinking alcohol example |
| **Principal letter (Sum Up #4)** | • Letter is addressed to the principal and is at least two paragraphs long |
| | • First paragraph introduces the problem and reviews the testing procedures |
| | • Second paragraph summarizes the results, includes quantitative support for the conclusion, and provides directions for using the bulb |

## Objective

The purpose of this experiment is to evaluate the effectiveness of a measurement tool using experimentation and the concept of density.

## Materials

- Common lab equipment
- Isopropyl alcohol
- Metric scale

- Energy drink, pop, or juice (Tea does not work well, and some carbonated beverages will not be as effective in this lab because the bubbles cause the balls to rise regardless of the density of the liquid.)

**Teaching Notes**

This lab was created using Chaslyn Antifreeze Testers ($0.97 each). These hydrometers have five colored balls that float differently based on the density of the solution. Hydrometers that have been used with actual antifreeze may respond differently than new ones because the balls behave somewhat differently once they have been coated with antifreeze. However, these differences will not reduce the overall effectiveness of this lab. This lab is ideal for students to test their skills of controlling variables and setting up "fair tests." Resist the urge to tell the students what to do. Let them make their own mistakes and develop their own procedures. They may redo parts of this lab multiple times, and the materials are not dangerous, so let them go.

Throughout this activity, remind students to record their data to reinforce their results as reported to the principal (Sum Up #4).

Each ball has a different density, so each floats/sinks according to the density of the solution in which it is suspended. Adding alcohol to common drinks will dramatically reduce the density (the density of pure alcohol is approximately 0.88 g/mL) and cause fewer balls (or none) to float. Student answers will vary; examples include testing antifreeze, the sugar content of wine, and the salinity of fish tanks.

## *Scores and Explanation*

The Booze Bulb task receives the highest scores for all three standards. For construction of knowledge, students develop procedures for inquiry, organize and analyze data, make conclusions, evaluate the usefulness of the tool, and write scientific reports. That is, the task demands very little reproduction of knowledge or processes; almost all of the students' work is original.

For elaborated scientific communication (disciplined inquiry), students draw conclusions from their inquiry about the concept of density and efficacy of a specific measurement tool. In addition, the task asks them to support their conclusions by presenting data and explaining answers to the questions: Does the bulb work with all types of drinks? What is the minimum amount of alcohol it will detect? Finally, students write a brief letter to the school principal, making their case for the Booze Bulb based on the results of their experiments.

Task expectations in the letter to the principal meet the highest level of the rubric for value beyond school: influencing an audience beyond school. Though influencing the principal is technically not "beyond school," we give credit for a task that clearly intends for students' work to have value or meaning besides fulfilling requirements for the teacher or class. In different parts of the task, students also apply scientific knowledge and procedures to address a real problem and consider other potential useful applications of the Booze Bulb tool. In doing so, we infer that students are likely to better understand the utility of science in the real world.

---

In Part II, we have discussed the scoring of exemplary artifacts in different subjects and grade levels to elaborate on the three main criteria for Authentic Intellectual Work and to provide a foundation for the critical, collective inquiry teachers conduct in AIW teams. In Part III, we turn to enhancing teachers' capacities to implement AIW standards in their instruction and assessment practices through specific approaches to professional development.

# Part III
## Implementation That Builds Capacity

The research on existing practice shows strong relationships between authentic instruction and higher and more equitable student achievement. In Chapter 5, we describe research showing that some teachers' pedagogy is consistent enough with the Authentic Intellectual Work (AIW) standards to advance student achievement, despite their not having participated in professional development intentionally designed to implement the AIW framework. These teachers often described their teaching as "inquiry," "teaching for understanding," "problem-based learning," or helping students to "apply their learning." Others relied on subject area standards or approaches such as scientific inquiry, thinking like a historian, or cognitively guided instruction in math. Still, few teachers offer lessons consistent with AIW standards, and the majority of students are deprived of learning opportunities that promote high-quality intellectual work.

Therefore the next logical step should be to support teachers to deliberately promote Authentic Intellectual Work in their instruction and assessment practices. Can AIW professional development improve teacher learning and practice? If so, how can schools build capacity to sustain teaching for AIW over time?

In 2007, we partnered with the Iowa Department of Education to initiate AIW professional development in nine high schools. We drew on lessons from prior AIW professional development in a few schools as well as the emerging consensus in the field around effective professional development. To help teachers in Iowa consider whether, and how, to pursue professional development for AIW, we published *Authentic Instruction and Achievement: Common Standards for Rigor and Relevance in Teaching Academic Subjects* (Newmann, King, & Carmichael, 2007).

At first, it was unclear how many schools would choose to participate in the professional development partnership and how long the initiative would last. After a successful pilot year, however, word began to spread. Each year more schools expressed interest, and by 2015, thousands of teachers and administrators from more than 200 schools were engaged in AIW reform at varying stages of implementation. Most of these schools are in Iowa, but other promising partnerships are emerging elsewhere, including Connecticut, Georgia, Minnesota, and Wisconsin. These professional development experiences provide a solid foundation for identifying and resolving major implementation issues. In Part III, we outline how AIW professional development can successfully address these issues.

The focus of Chapter 6 is AIW reform at the school level. It identifies common questions teachers have about how AIW will help their teaching and recommends the roles and responsibilities for school building administrators to support them. We describe important issues faced before implementation as well as the structures and resources necessary to build well-functioning AIW teams within a school. Chapter 6 also proposes critical conditions to which schools should commit before engaging in AIW reform.

In Chapter 7, we discuss external roles and responsibilities to support teaching according to the AIW framework. This further explains the philosophy and approach that the Center for AIW uses to build local capacity to sustain teaching for AIW. We discuss how district central office administrators, as well as those in regional and statewide agencies, can support AIW reform in schools and help to expand beyond pilot schools. The lessons learned and insights offered about how districts, states, and other external agencies can sustain and expand initial efforts in schools are informed by current national debates and other research on how to scale up a successful reform.

# Chapter 5
## AIW Research

**OVERVIEW**

As part of the rationale for instruction grounded in Authentic Intellectual Work (AIW), Chapter 1 summarized research showing that students of teachers who score high on AIW criteria achieve at much higher levels than students of teachers whose instruction scores lower on the AIW criteria. The achievement benefits occurred on both conventional standardized tests and assessments of Authentic Intellectual Work.

This chapter's account of the research

- presents comprehensive evidence of AIW effectiveness in diverse contexts, regardless of students' race/ethnicity, socioeconomic status, gender, and prior academic achievement;

- explains how, by focusing on intellectual demands rather than teaching techniques or curriculum content, the research leaves decisions on these issues up to the professional discretion of teachers;

- explains how and why teaching according to the AIW framework seems to boost student achievement, which deepens understanding of the compelling results from the studies; and

- describes evidence of AIW teaching contributing to equity, that is, not only improved overall achievement but also reducing achievement gaps between students of lower and higher socioeconomic status and students with and without disabilities.

Combined with the foundation offered in Chapter 1, and elaborated through the examples in Chapters 2–4, this chapter should better equip teachers and administrators to take the implementation steps described in Chapters 6 and 7.

**SCOPE OF THE RESEARCH**

The original research on Authentic Intellectual Work occurred in schools throughout the United States from 1990 to 2003.[1] This research studied whether students who experienced instruction and assessment that promoted higher levels of AIW showed higher achievement than students who experienced lower levels of instruction and assessment aimed toward AIW. The studies also explored what conditions within schools and beyond seemed to help and hinder schools' promotion of AIW. Findings were published as early as 1995, but not until the work with Iowa in 2007 did systematic large-scale professional development, described later in this chapter, help teachers apply the findings.

Data on instruction were collected in more than 1,100 schools and 1,600 classes in different communities throughout the United States, along with achievement data from more than 19,000 diverse students in these settings in Grades 3–12. The studies demonstrated that students who experienced higher levels of authentic instruction and assessment showed higher achievement than students who experienced lower levels of authentic instruction and assessment. The results were consistent for Grades 3–12, across different subject areas (mathematics, social studies, language arts, science), and regardless of students' race, gender, or socioeconomic status.

All of the studies assessed the extent to which teachers promoted Authentic Intellectual Work through classroom instruction and assignments given to students. Studies varied in the subject areas and grade levels examined as well as in the type of achievement measured. For example, some studies measured student performance according to criteria for AIW demonstrated in student written work for teachers' assignments. Others measured student performance on conventional tests of basic skills and retention of knowledge. The original research also addressed the issue of equity by assessing the influence of students' social backgrounds (socioeconomic status, race, gender) and prior school achievement on the connection between classroom promotion of AIW and student performance. Since 2003, additional studies have examined the extent of authentic pedagogy in classrooms, both in the United States and abroad, as well as its connection to student achievement and equity.

## MOVING FROM TEACHING PRACTICES TO INTELLECTUAL DEMANDS

When educators, the public, or researchers want to improve teaching, they typically try to identify "best practices," or "what works," and then attempt to implement those through professional development or preservice education. Examples of practices considered effective include direct instruction, thematic or interdisciplinary learning, cooperative learning, student journals, the project method, hands-on activities, tutoring, portfolio assessment, role-playing/simulation, multimedia presentations, web-based learning programs, and student discussions.

Research may have shown some practices to be more effective than others for teaching specific skills or content to a specific group of students, but no single practice or set of practices has been shown to be most effective for varied intellectual outcomes for most students across several grade levels and subjects. The absence of universally effective teaching practices is probably due to the fact that any given teaching method can usually be used to cultivate intellectual work ranging from low to high quality. A teacher could replace lecture or recitation with small-group discussion, or short-answer worksheets with essay questions. But even with these changes, students might still devote most of their efforts to remembering and listing isolated pieces of information, rather than thinking critically about how the information helps them understand a powerful idea or solve an important problem. A portfolio that shows a variety of student work over a semester might replace the final examination taken in one sitting, but the portfolio itself could be filled with entries that fail to show in-depth understanding of the subject. Conversely, a high-quality lecture/discussion or a carefully constructed short-answer homework question could lead students to use a few key ideas to develop in-depth and complex understanding of an issue.

According to the AIW framework, the merit of any practice or technique, whether conventional or innovative, should be judged on the extent to which it makes intellectual demands consistent with AIW. To study the extent of AIW in schools and what teachers do to promote it, we developed standards and rubrics, not for describing teachers' specific teaching techniques, but instead for *the quality of intellectual work they encourage, regardless of their techniques or practices.* Some practices undoubtedly give more opportunity for certain kinds of intellectual work to occur. For example, discussions and essays give more opportunity for students to explain themselves than lectures or multiple-choice questions, but knowing only that discussion occurred or essays were assigned gives no assurance that the teacher used these practices to generate elaborated student explanations. Furthermore, it is unclear whether the students are elaborating on their own arguments and conclusions or simply restating evidence or positions discussed in class. Likewise, lectures and multiple-choice questions help deliver and check for student acquisition of facts and foundational knowledge but offer no guarantee that students can use such knowledge to solve problems or make defensible inferences.

## METHOD AND RESULTS

According to eight main studies that examined effects of authentic pedagogy, students who experienced higher levels of instruction and assessment showed higher achievement than students who experienced lower levels of instruction and assessment aimed toward Authentic Intellectual Work, independent of the influence of students' race, gender, socioeconomic status, or prior achievement. The achievement benefits occurred on both direct assessments of authentic intellectual performance and conventional standardized tests of basic skills and curriculum content across all grades and all subjects studied. Figures A.1 and A.2 in the Appendix provide details of the studies, but we summarize their results here.

In the five studies that examined student achievement using criteria for Authentic Intellectual Work based on AIW rubrics to score student writing in the four main subjects, the average achievement benefit to students in higher versus lower scoring teachers' classes averaged 42 percentile points (Appendix, Figure A.1). In the three studies that examined student achievement using conventional standardized tests of basic skills, the average achievement benefit to students in higher versus lower scoring teachers' classes averaged 49 percentile points (Appendix, Figure A.2).

## A CLOSER LOOK AT TWO STUDIES

### The CORS Study of Authentic Achievement

From 1990 to 1995, the Center on Organization and Restructuring of Schools (CORS) studied three mathematics and three social studies classes in eight elementary schools, eight middle schools, and eight high schools across the United States that were making significant efforts in "restructuring" their schools. For each teacher, four lessons per year were observed and rated on standards for authentic instruction.[2] In addition, each teacher submitted four assignments that she or he considered to pose challenging assessments of students' understanding of the subject. The teachers also submitted the students' written work in response to the assignments. Researchers and practicing teachers not participating in the study scored the quality of assignments and student work according to standards for authentic assignments and for authentic student work. Thus, each class received an *authentic pedagogy* score based on lesson observations and assignment quality. Each class also received an average authentic performance score based on the quality of student work. Figure 5.1 indicates the average performance score of students, on a scale of 3–12, whose classes received low, average, and high authentic pedagogy scores. The difference in scores between 5.4 and 6.8 represents 30 percentile points in the full distribution of scores.

**Figure 5.1 Mathematics and Social Studies Authentic Student Performance in Classes With Low, Average, and High Authentic Pedagogy**

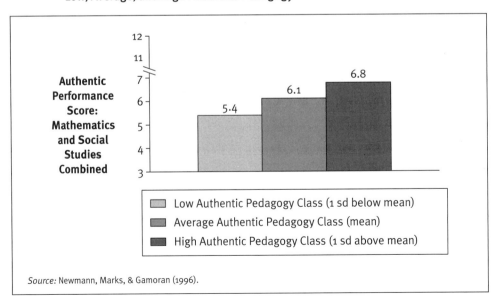

Source: Newmann, Marks, & Gamoran (1996).

## The Chicago Study of Conventional Academic Achievement

From 1996 to 1999, 46 Chicago elementary schools with grades K–8 participated in this study. Teachers of language arts and mathematics in Grades 3, 6, and 8 submitted six student assignments per year, two of which they considered to pose challenging assessments of the students' understanding of the subject.[3] They also submitted students' written work in response to the assignments.[4] Chicago teachers of language arts and mathematics at each of the grade levels who did not participate in the study scored the quality of teachers' assignments and student written work according to the standards for authentic assignments and authentic student work. For the Iowa Test of Basic Skills (ITBS), given to all students in Chicago, students' gain scores for each of 3 years were averaged for each of the teachers' classes. Using the average gain in basic skills across all Chicago schools in each subject and grade as the reference point (1-year ITBS gain), Figure 5.2 compares the gains in basic skills for students receiving assignments scored in the highest versus lowest quartile of the 46 schools. Students receiving higher quality assignments gained about 20% more in basic skills than the Chicago average gain and almost 40% more than students receiving the lowest quality assignments.

**Figure 5.2** Students' Gains in Reading and Mathematics on the ITBS According to Quality of Teachers' Assignments in Writing and Mathematics

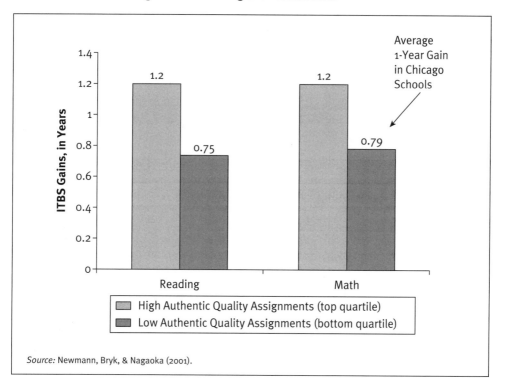

Source: Newmann, Bryk, & Nagaoka (2001).

## Explaining the Findings

Authentic instruction probably boosts student achievement on measures of AIW and on more conventional standardized tests through different processes. Higher performance can be explained in part by extensive other research showing strong connections between teachers' expectations and student achievement: High teacher expectations lead to high achievement, low expectations to low achievement.[5] Since observers of teaching usually find pervasive skepticism in teachers and the public that educationally disadvantaged students of limited academic ability can meet the intellectually complex and rigorous challenges posed by criteria for AIW, it was particularly instructive (and for some even surprising) to learn that students of all social backgrounds and levels of prior achievement benefited from demands for AIW.

Explaining positive results on authentic measures of achievement seems reasonably straightforward—if teachers demand AIW, they probably try to help students produce it. In other words, when teachers' lessons and tasks require higher order thinking, deeper learning of important content, and application of academic learning to diverse situations beyond school, diverse students are more likely to succeed on tests that assess these qualities. One still might wonder how the intellectual demands of authentic instruction enhance achievement on conventional standardized tests that usually do not demand AIW. Conventional wisdom suggests that basic skills and key information in subject areas are best taught through drill and practice; that is, unless these skills are explicitly taught and memorized, students, especially those from disadvantaged backgrounds, are unlikely to succeed on tests of basic skills or on standardized tests of subject matter content. Such conventional wisdom can make teachers reluctant to demand construction of knowledge and in-depth understanding through elaborated communication because they may feel these demands take instructional time away from directly covering all the facts and skills that might be required on a test.

We explain the fact that students of teachers who make higher demands for AIW actually perform better on conventional tests of basic skills and knowledge than students of teachers who make lower demands for AIW in two ways.

First, conventional standardized tests put tremendous emphasis on *mastery of vocabulary*. Even when the questions do not appear to be tests of vocabulary, these tests are in large part assessments of students' knowledge of the meaning of words. This is especially common in conventional tests of reading, though it applies to other subjects as well. For example, writing tests assess students' proper use of words in sentences and paragraphs to convey students' intended meaning. Writing skills and rules of grammar, such as knowing how to frame a topic sentence or the difference between subject and verb, require student understanding of words. In the case of mathematics and science tests, in order to score well students must execute operations or choose answers that show an understanding of "vocabulary" such as addition, division, perimeter, percent, velocity, and temperature. As explained below, demands for Authentic Intellectual

Work can lead to increased vocabulary competence, even though vocabulary may not be taught explicitly through traditional methods.

When teachers demand AIW, they may use extensive drill and recitation less often to teach the meaning of words or basic bits of knowledge. Instead, they may require students to think about and use words and concepts to solve problems that have personal meaning. When students construct knowledge through disciplined inquiry, they often must consider alternative solutions; justify their conclusions with reasons and evidence; apply their knowledge to new contexts; develop deep understanding of topics, rather than only superficial awareness; and express themselves through elaborated communication, rather than in terse linguistic fragments.

In one way or another, these intellectual tasks emphasize extensive use and application of words and ideas in varied contexts. As students study a topic in some depth, the rules, algorithms, and words they learn are less likely to be memorized as disconnected skills and facts, and more likely to be integrated within larger cognitive schema that connect new bits of information to one another and to students' prior knowledge. Since cognitively integrated knowledge is more readily internalized and retained by students, it is more likely to be remembered and correctly applied on standardized tests than knowledge memorized as discrete items only for the purpose of repeating it when called on (see Bransford, Brown, & Cocking, 2000).

The illustration conveys a second part of our explanation: *Participation in authentic intellectual activity helps to motivate and sustain students in the hard work that learning requires.* Since demands for AIW pose questions of interest to students in their lives beyond school, students are more likely to care about both the questions they study and

---

### Illustration

Ninth-grade math students worked in groups on the "staircase problem" in which they attempted to find the rule or generalization to predict the number of square blocks necessary for a staircase of any number of steps. "Is it a two-step answer for the rule?" pleaded one student early on. "Maybe," replied her teacher, who throughout the lesson refused to make the task any easier. After numerous attempts and growing frustration, one group's determined efforts seemed to be paying off. "Okay, you try to make it a square, right," exclaimed one student. "You have a three by three," she continued, laying out cutout blocks on their paper. "Which equals nine [blocks] . . . then you minus the number you used to get it." "But that wouldn't work for every rule," another group member responded. "You have to think of a different rule for odd numbers and even numbers." The first student chimed back, her voice rising, thinking she was on to something, "Wait a minute. Oh! Oh! Wait, wait, wait." "I hate this. Every time I think I know what the answer is, it doesn't work!" a third student exclaimed. The first student declared, "EXACTLY. It drives me insane." But they persisted.

*Source:* http://learner.org/resources/series34.html (#6 The Staircase Problem)

the answers they learn. Thus, such assignments enhance a student's willingness to put forth serious effort in learning the material, as compared with exercises that have no personal meaning beyond completing an assignment to please the teacher or to attain a promotion. In sum, assignments that demand more AIW elicit intensive thinking about and deeper engagement in varied applications of words, concepts, and ideas. This can help students internalize understandings as their own and use this knowledge to respond to items on conventional tests that may not have been explicitly covered in class.

## Authentic Instruction Enhances Educational Equity

Evidence from the studies supports four findings related to equity in education:

- Authentic instruction and assignments bring significant benefits to students of any race, ethnicity, socioeconomic status (SES), or gender. Although students with higher prior academic achievement derive slightly greater benefit from authentic instruction and assignments, these benefits are minimal compared with the robust benefits that students from all racial, SES, and gender groups experience.

- Secondary students with mild to moderate learning disabilities in inclusive classes benefit substantially from authentic assignments on assessments of authentic intellectual performance (see Appendix, Figures A.1, A.5). As might be expected, students without disabilities did better across all classes, but importantly, students with disabilities who received higher levels of authentic pedagogy produced more authentic work than students with or without disabilities who received lower levels of authentic pedagogy.

- Student exposure to high levels of authentic instruction can be distributed equally to students of any race, ethnicity, SES, or gender. In the group of schools studied, whether students received higher or lower levels of authentic instruction was not related to any of these student background factors.

- Authentic instruction can help to reduce the link between students' social background and academic achievement. The National Educational Longitudinal Study, a large national study of high school students, found that in schools with higher levels of authentic instruction, the connection between students' SES and scores on conventional achievement tests such as the National Assessment of Educational Progress (NAEP) was weaker than in schools with lower levels of authentic instruction. It also found that the gap in achievement gains from Grades 8–12 between students with high and low SES decreased substantially in schools with high levels of authentic instruction, but the achievement gap between SES groups increased in schools with low levels of authentic instruction. While stronger demands for Authentic Intellectual Work did not eliminate the achievement gap, it decreased it (Lee & Smith, 1996).[6] Further, the

CORS study found that the effect of students' social background on measures of authentic achievement seems to be less than the effect of social background on conventional achievement tests. Newmann et al. (1996) found that on the measure of authentic achievement across elementary, middle, and high schools, Hispanics and students with low SES did not score significantly lower than Whites or students with high SES, while African Americans scored lower than Whites and girls scored higher than boys. But the gap in authentic performance between African Americans and Whites or between boys and girls was no greater, and quite possibly less, than the gap on the more traditional NAEP measure that was used as a pretest.

These findings show that authentic instruction does not exacerbate, and often helps reduce, gaps in student achievement attributable to students' demographic backgrounds, or learning disabilities, which helps to advance equity. Unfortunately, since most studies found wide variation between classes within schools, wide variation between schools in the levels of authentic instruction offered, and overall low levels of authentic instruction, most schools are still a long way from offering authentic instruction to all.[7]

## FROM RESEARCH ON EXISTING PRACTICE TO PROFESSIONAL DEVELOPMENT FOR AIW

Results of the original research were significant, not only because of the consistency of positive findings among several different studies but also because the studies used common rubrics to describe intellectual demands across several subjects and grade levels, and they focused on intellectual work that teachers demand and students carry out in classrooms rather than specific teaching practices. Because the research depended on these latter two strategies, we believed that teachers and administrators would welcome efforts to implement the framework.

Still, the studies summarized here did not evaluate programs to help teachers deliberately use criteria for AIW. Instead, the purpose of the research was to see whether criteria for authentic instruction and student work when used to assess existing practice, without teachers' knowledge of the criteria, would suggest guidelines for improving the intellectual quality of teaching and student achievement. In the original research we did not share the language of the AIW framework or the specific rubrics for evaluating instruction and achievement. In describing their teaching, teachers used language such as *inquiry, teaching students to think, teaching for understanding*, and helping students *apply their learning*, but they did not reference the language of the framework or its specific standards to describe their work.

After several years of research on existing practice in different contexts showed strong relationships between authentic instruction and student achievement, the next logical step was to help teachers deliberately promote AIW. Following publication of the original research in 1995, CORS staff members participated in several workshops to explain research results and criteria to teachers and administrators nationwide, and in a few schools we offered coaching and other professional development, but not on a large scale in districts or states until 2007.

## Evaluation of Professional Development for AIW, 2007–2011

From 2007 to 2014, the Iowa Department of Education sponsored statewide professional development across the state to help teachers design instruction and assessments that increase student Authentic Intellectual Work. By 2012, the AIW professional development project was the largest Iowa Department of Education–supported professional development initiative in the state. The initial evaluation[8] described the project's impact in several areas:

- the professional development process in schools, through case studies of implementation in four schools

- administrators' reactions to the project, through focus group discussions with administrators and curriculum directors

- the extent to which teachers' intellectual demands were affected by professional development that emphasizes feedback from colleagues on the quality of their learning tasks for students, through an analysis that compared task quality before and after receiving collegial feedback

- whether participation in the AIW project was associated with higher student achievement on the Iowa Test of Basic Skills and, for high school, the Iowa Test of Educational Development, through a comparison of test scores in AIW schools and scores of students in matched schools not in the project

### IMPACT OF AIW PROFESSIONAL DEVELOPMENT ON STUDENT ACHIEVEMENT

The original research on AIW focused on student achievement benefits. This section summarizes Iowa results related to that issue. The AIW-Iowa project to date has not been able to link individual students' scores to their teachers, record each teacher's actual level of participation in AIW professional development, or determine the quality of teachers' implementation of AIW standards.[9] The initial evaluation used a simpler design. The effect of AIW professional development on student performance was estimated by comparing student achievement in a sample of schools participating in the project (AIW schools) to the achievement in a matched sample of comparison schools not participating in AIW professional development.

The AIW schools selected for the study were those in which all teachers engaged in AIW as their primary professional development for one full year prior to the date of testing in 2010–2011. Given that condition, data from 16 schools representing 10 districts implementing AIW were used. These districts and schools were matched to another set of Iowa schools and districts not implementing AIW using the same grade structure and falling within 10% on each of the following variables: total student enrollment, percent White, percent low SES, percent English language learners, percent Individualized Education Plan. These criteria led to selection of 17 schools representing 12 districts as the non-AIW comparison schools.

Test data in 2010–2011 from the ITBS for Grades 3–8 and the Iowa Tests of Educational Development (ITED) in Grades 9–11 in reading, mathematics, science, and social studies were compared. Across all grades and subjects, the scores of a total of 3,908 students in the 16 AIW schools and 4,060 students in 17 non-AIW schools were compared.

Students in AIW schools across grade levels and subjects usually scored higher on the ITBS/ITED than students in non-AIW schools. AIW schools also had higher percentages of students scoring proficient. The results across all Grades 3–11 were similar. For Grades 4, 8, and 11—the grades for which Iowa schools must report annually—AIW students scored statistically significantly higher in 8 of the 12 comparisons (three grades in each of four subjects), and AIW students had higher percentages proficient in all 12 comparisons. The percentile advantage to AIW students was 5 points or higher in 8 of the 12 comparisons.[10] Students in AIW schools outperformed students in comparison schools most consistently in mathematics and least consistently in social studies.

The results, while encouraging, do not prove that AIW professional development caused student achievement benefits. An ideal design to estimate the effect of AIW professional development on student performance would include data on individual teachers' degree of participation in AIW professional development, the quality of participating teachers' implementation of AIW as measured by their scores on revised tasks, and a database that permitted the linking of test scores for specific students to their teachers. Such a design could show the effects of AIW professional development on teachers' practice and the effects of teachers' practice on student achievement.

While we were not able to use a more rigorous research design in the initial evaluation, after we saw its promising results, we decided to study whether advantages for AIW students might not have been due to participation in the AIW program, but instead to selection bias. This is a problem common to any intervention in which participation is voluntary; the volunteers might differ in important ways from those who do not participate even before an intervention begins. Perhaps teachers in the schools that volunteered to participate in AIW professional development might have been more highly motivated to devote serious effort to their students' achievement than teachers in non-AIW schools. If achievement results in the AIW schools prior to project entry were higher than in the comparison schools, this would certainly challenge conclusions that AIW professional development was responsible for the differences. We tested this explanation by examining achievement trends in AIW and matched non-AIW comparison schools prior to the AIW schools' participation in the AIW project. If the AIW and comparison schools did not differ in achievement prior to the start of AIW professional development, the professional development itself would likely have contributed to improved student achievement.

The initiative began in fall 2007. To determine whether the initial positive results were due to selection bias, we examined achievement data in reading and math in the same AIW and control schools for three years: 2004–2005, 2005–2006, and 2006–2007. The results indicate that in the 3 years prior to implementation, grade-level achievement in AIW schools was equivalent to non-AIW schools' achievement in 15 of the 18 comparisons (3 years x 3 grades x 2 subjects). In contrast, in 2010–2011, after the project had been in effect, AIW achievement exceeded non-AIW achievement in 5 of the 6 comparisons (1 year x 3 grades x 2 subjects). Since AIW and comparison schools' achievement did not differ substantially prior to project entry, but AIW students' achievement exceeded comparison students following project entry, we conclude that selection bias does not explain the 2010–2011 achievement differences, and a reasonable case can be made that the differences were due to the AIW professional development.

## IMPACT OF AIW PROFESSIONAL DEVELOPMENT ON TEACHERS' PRACTICE AND SCHOOL CULTURE

The observations, interviews and focus groups, and case studies indicate consistent positive results for teachers and students as well as challenges that need further attention.

### Impact on Teachers' Practice

Focus groups and case studies described the changing nature of instruction from the teacher as deliverer of facts to the teacher as facilitator of student thinking, in-depth understanding, and skill development that is meaningful and valuable. The quality of classroom discussions became much deeper and more thoughtful. Expectations for students were increased and curriculum more closely connected to students' lives, making lessons more challenging and, simultaneously, more meaningful. Because students were more engaged, they were more persistent in problem solving.

A close look at the quality of tasks teachers assigned to students also showed positive results. The evaluation analyzed 112 original and revised tasks from high school teachers in the four subject areas of English/language arts, math, science, and social studies. Since the AIW project initially focused on secondary schools, evaluators chose task samples only from high school. The review of teachers' tasks showed that high school teachers who participated in AIW professional development did revise and implement assessment tasks that scored higher in the standards for authenticity. Statistically significant increases occurred for three of the four subject areas, with effect sizes ranging from medium in science and social studies to large in mathematics.[11]

## Change in Professional Culture and Leadership

Administrators referred to the level of collaboration among teachers as "unprecedented." Teams of teachers, using common protocols and criteria, met within and across disciplines to improve their practices. Teachers examined their practices through the AIW framework, individually and collectively asking questions such as the following: "Will this lesson provoke students' higher order thinking and substantive conversation?" "Does this unit lead students to apply and understand knowledge in contexts beyond school?" "Will this assessment task require students to show in-depth understanding of an important concept?" Teachers valued the opportunities AIW professional development provided to improve their instruction as well as the leadership opportunities it provided them. AIW schools also experienced more sustained focus for their professional development. Because administrators were part of the learning team, they found themselves giving teachers more relevant feedback, and overall, AIW improved the collaborative spirit between administrators and teachers.

### CONCLUSION

The framework for AIW along with the research should encourage teachers and administrators to implement the AIW framework through systematic professional development. The rubrics for scoring instruction, assignments, and student work described in Chapters 2–4 have been used successfully when teachers and administrators work hard to apply the framework in their particular contexts. Since the AIW framework does not include curriculum material or instruments to measure student achievement, teachers and administrators must continue to make decisions about what curriculum content to include and how to find or develop appropriate materials and activities for instruction and assessment. Chapters 6 and 7 address specific concerns of teachers and administrators and describe the roles they need to assume, the organizational structures to support, and the resources needed to maximize success.

# Chapter 6
## Internal Support

*Building Capacity for Improved Teaching in Schools*

## OVERVIEW

We know from years of failed initiatives, reform du jour approaches, and pendulum swings that teaching is much the same as it's always been. According to educational historian Larry Cuban (2013), the most persistent trend has been incremental modification without fundamental reform. Similarly, Richard Elmore (2000) showed that leaders "tinker" around the edges of the core technologies of schooling—teaching and learning—and rarely work effectively to improve instruction.

In contrast, Authentic Intellectual Work (AIW) professional development aims toward fundamental change in instruction and assessment that advances learning for all students. Because the AIW framework requires such a shift in thinking about instruction, once teachers and administrators decide to begin serious consideration of AIW, a number of important issues need to be faced. In this chapter, we first address teachers' concerns that may lead them to resist AIW professional development (PD) and implementation of the AIW framework. We then outline our approach to professional development that has contributed to teacher learning and improvement in their practices.

## TEACHER CONCERNS—IS AIW FOR ME?

After being introduced to AIW through reading or an initial orientation, many teachers enthusiastically embrace the opportunity to collaboratively examine their practice and develop common understanding by using the criteria of the AIW framework to improve student learning. Other teachers are more hesitant, and over the past decade they have raised concerns that we address here. We offer answers to common questions, but ultimately, teacher commitment comes mainly from engaging in the work and experiencing positive results with students and colleagues.

### Why do I need this?

Students from diverse backgrounds benefit from teachers who deliberately use AIW standards to guide lesson planning and learning tasks. Numerous research studies show that without professional development on AIW, teaching with high levels of Authentic

Intellectual Work can occur, although unfortunately it is rare. Since definitions of high-quality intellectual work are varied or vague, many teachers may perceive their teaching as effective, even though their standards for success rarely match AIW criteria. Teachers who excel in teaching most students and who unconsciously meet some of the criteria for AIW are intrigued when introduced to the AIW framework and often wish to learn more about it.

Without careful study of the approach, some teachers assume they already teach according to the standards in the AIW framework because they favor student-centered classrooms and discussion. Others make that assumption because they emphasize student portfolios or rubrics, independent and cooperative student projects, or because they use "the inquiry method," Bloom's taxonomy, or some other approach that seems consistent with the Authentic Intellectual Work framework. Or teachers using the Common Core State Standards may believe they need no further professional development to improve their teaching.

Existing instructional activities or programs may share common elements with AIW, but careful analysis usually reveals critical differences. For example, some teachers may emphasize *construction of knowledge* and *higher order thinking* but neglect *elaborated communication,* an important dimension of *disciplined inquiry,* without which students' original thinking remains superficial. Student-centered classrooms and AIW both emphasize problems of interest to students, but student-centered classrooms don't necessarily insist on the degree of intellectual rigor that AIW demands. Whenever teachers claim they already teach according to AIW standards, we have always found opportunities for them to improve. As one principal said, "AIW makes my best teachers even better." The question becomes: How much energy are they willing to devote to an AIW reform effort? This issue should be discussed so that informed decisions are made before a staff commits to ongoing professional development to implement the AIW approach.

## Nice idea, but isn't AIW too difficult for many students?

Another barrier to AIW reform can be low teacher expectations of student ability. Teachers may be convinced of the value of AIW as a central educational goal but see their students as incapable of accomplishing complex intellectual work. Teachers may believe that students first need to learn more basic knowledge and skills through traditional presentations and practice. This widespread concern should always be challenged for two reasons:

- The "facts first" belief that students should not be challenged to think until they have learned all the relevant facts can prevent students from ever being challenged with more complex work, because the supply of knowledge relevant to complex questions is continually growing and is, in essence, infinite. Not even the most educated, experienced person will ever master all relevant knowledge before being called upon to think and draw conclusions. The persisting intellectual challenge for students of all ages and adults alike is to reach defensible conclusions in spite of usually incomplete knowledge.

- Research described in Chapter 5 shows that in many cases it is unnecessary to teach basic knowledge and skills separately prior to posing authentic intellectual challenges. Studies of national samples and in Chicago found that improvement in basic knowledge and skills is greater for students of teachers who emphasize Authentic Intellectual Work. Compared to teaching the "basics" through drill and practice of decontextualized bits of knowledge and isolated skills, teaching toward Authentic Intellectual Work involves meaningful discussion and reasoning about diverse content. This approach is more likely to boost retention and transfer of basic vocabulary and communication skills. Roland Case (2013) concisely summarized the research on this issue: "Let's recognize that rigorous thinking is how we learn. Transmitting information and providing definitions don't develop factual and conceptual understanding. This is more likely to develop by problematizing the content using 'higher order' learning tasks so that students are engaged in digesting the material" (p. 199).

## Won't most students resist more intellectually challenging work?

Teachers commonly worry that students would not be interested in more intellectually challenging work. Many students, especially those from dominant cultural and advantaged economic backgrounds, have learned the "rules of game" and are adept at getting the "right answers" and meeting traditional expectations for learning. Some students, accustomed to more traditional didactic teaching, may initially resist AIW demands for the increased effort required by critical thinking, conceptual understanding, and elaborated communication. These students may initially balk because they do not have the skills or dispositions for risk taking and complex thinking. Yet after a few months of careful implementation, teachers tend to agree that teaching for AIW boosts student engagement.

While we can cannot scientifically demonstrate how AIW enhances student engagement, more opportunities to contribute ideas and make meaning while constructing knowledge about issues or problems outside of school appears to increase student interest and willingness to put forth the effort that learning requires. This is probably due to more opportunities for students to apply their own thoughts, developed through discussions and writing backed by academic knowledge, in order to solve problems that have meaning beyond compliance with teachers' instructions. Since teaching toward Authentic Intellectual Work is also more likely to boost student achievement on tests that demand Authentic Intellectual Work and on tests of retention and transfer of basic vocabulary and communication skills, students' greater academic success may also enhance their engagement in learning.

## Does AIW rule out all "traditional" teaching?

It is realistically impossible and probably educationally unwise for even the most gifted teachers with the most gifted students to abandon all traditional teaching and to replace it with authentic teaching for every part of every lesson. Sufficiently enriched instructional materials do not exist, and some knowledge and skills are more efficiently learned through traditional intellectual demands for recall, routine application of algorithms, and simple reporting of what has been learned.

The goal of professional development for AIW is to increase opportunities for students to engage in Authentic Intellectual Work, which, for teachers, can mean simply striving for a better balance between traditional teaching and Authentic Intellectual Work. The idea is to increase demands for Authentic Intellectual Work, though in manageable incremental steps focused on concepts and units of study that lend themselves to teaching consistent with the AIW framework.

In setting professional goals, teachers engaged in AIW should discuss options for increasing this balance. For example, if students currently spend only about 15%–20% of their time doing Authentic Intellectual Work, over a 3-year period of professional development on an AIW team, might it be reasonable to increase that percentage to 50%? The challenge for teachers is to continuously examine curriculum and learning goals and ask themselves: Which goals can best be pursued through students producing Authentic Intellectual Work, and which can best be taught only through more traditional didactic methods?

## Will the AIW framework address persistent challenges in teachers' work?

Teachers commonly face difficult challenges. Some conditions, such as large class sizes or students with diverse needs, skills, and motivation, prevent teachers from giving individual students the attention they need. Other challenges to teachers' professional work include demands to teach too much material, lack of time to share expertise with colleagues, pressure to ensure that students score well on external tests, and pressure to implement diverse professional development initiatives that change from year to year. Teachers need to feel confident that committing time and effort to a proposed initiative will help them address some of their difficulties.

The AIW framework offers no panacea for all these issues. School, district, and state leadership must address policies, including resource allocation, that result in large classes, insufficient planning time, broad content coverage, and excessive pressure to succeed on achievement tests of questionable value. While it offers no complete solutions, AIW professional development can help address the following issues.

- *Professional rewards:* Teachers who practice high levels of authentic pedagogy motivate students by offering them opportunities to think about, understand,

and apply academic knowledge to real-world concerns, instead of mechanically memorizing and reproducing isolated bits of knowledge used only in school. As teachers engage students in AIW, teachers themselves tend to find teaching and professional relationships more interesting and rewarding.

- *In-depth curriculum:* The AIW framework does not specify what curriculum content ought to be taught in a subject or at a grade level. But the importance it places on depth of understanding within disciplined inquiry, along with research indicating achievement benefits of depth over coverage, should support teachers' decisions to cover less content. In choosing from the vast array of curriculum content to include for in-depth study, we recommend that teachers select content that (1) is significant in a discipline or essential to studying a significant issue or topic, (2) has high potential for teaching authentically as described in the three AIW criteria, (3) is of interest to the teacher and understood by him or her in depth, and (4) is aligned with some *rigorous learning outcomes* specified by the school, external standards (such as anchor standards of the Common Core State Standards), or tests.

- *Coherent PD:* Teachers bombarded from year to year by diverse and changing professional development initiatives will question the value of devoting sustained time to any of them, suspecting that the latest new initiative will eventually be replaced by another fad. While the AIW framework alone cannot reduce the number of different professional development activities teachers are urged or required to attend, Chapter 7 suggests how school leadership and other education agencies can narrow the range of professional development so that AIW can be sustained as the central focus.

## Perspective From Practice

Allison Berryhill, English and Journalism Teacher, Atlantic High School, Atlantic, IA

*I believe that too often teachers (myself included) think we're pretty good at our jobs—or good enough. This attitude is a matter of self preservation. After all, who wants to end each day thinking we're not good at our jobs? No one. Therefore, we're quick to forgive our sloppy teaching, negligent in scrutinizing our students' true level of learning, and inflated in our sense of our success. AIW asks us to hold ourselves to a higher standard. I appreciate how AIW has pushed me to prioritize what I know in my gut is good teaching.*

*An example of AIW awareness impacting my teaching happened last week. I am not a teacher who lectures often or for long stretches of class. But when I do lecture, I like to think I'm pretty good at it. I'm an energized speaker, I know how to use examples, I interject questions, I incorporate good visual and audio aids. So it is tempting for me to think my students are "getting" what I'm lecturing about, especially if they are looking alert, nodding at appropriate times, and taking notes.*

*My class, in an unspoken alliance to play the school game, seems to know that when I ask a question, someone should pipe up with an answer, to reinforce my feeling that the whole class is following along.*

*But thanks to AIW, I was aware that my students' answers were not building on each other. I knew that my teaching would be better if I paused for "Turn to your neighbor and explain . . ." to get a higher level of sustained conversation.*

*What happened surprised me: My students turned to each other and said, "Beats me," "No idea," "Guess I wasn't paying attention." What a wallop! My perception had been that they were learning; the reality was that they were not. How often does this "teaching" go on in classrooms?*

*I made immediate adjustments. I said, "After this next slide, I'll ask you to talk about why this event matters in the history of journalism." Simply prepping my students in that way improved their absorption of the content. This is such a small thing, yet it greatly improved the lesson. I also put another check mark in the Don't Resort to Lecture column.*

## IMPLEMENTING AIW PROFESSIONAL DEVELOPMENT

Having decided to participate in AIW professional development, the first step is to form at least one team of *pilot teachers* in a school. Some teachers initially interested in AIW may wish to avoid involvement with colleagues outside their disciplines or grade levels, or simply prefer to work alone. Few students will benefit unless teachers promote AIW together in teams. The AIW team process depends on colleagues reviewing each other's work and challenging each other, an activity that obviously cannot be done alone. For example, the Art task presented in Chapter 3 resulted from Mr. Thompson bringing a version of this task to his colleagues for improvement. A team scoring and discussion session offered him specific feedback, which he used to revise the task and use with students in the future.

Providing opportunities for all teachers in a school to engage in AIW is critical to ensure that all students eventually have access to authentic learning. But in the first 1 to 3 years after a school begins to implement the AIW framework, the focus of professional development should be limited to an initial team or a few teams concentrating on building teacher and administrator capacity to work with the AIW framework. After successful implementation on a small scale with one or a few teams in a school, expansion can proceed to a whole school and/or more schools.

Ideally, expansion would extend to a whole district or region so that teams and schools become nested within a larger administrative and policy environment that sustains and expands application of the framework. But we strongly caution against premature expansion. Too many reform efforts have failed because schools try to scale up too quickly. Before expanding beyond the initial small-scale pilot, AIW educators must learn enough and experience sufficient positive results to have confidence that expansion is justified. For this reason, we advocate that schools start with one or two teams and then judiciously expand so that the staff builds sufficient capacity to use AIW successfully beyond the pilot.

Pilot team activities focus on building the competence of each teacher to teach according to the AIW framework by scoring and revising her or his own lessons, tasks, and assessments. Beyond building individual teacher competence, each team must aim toward building capacity within and beyond the team to use the framework successfully enough to decrease future reliance on support from external sources. To increase the likelihood of early success, we recommend that schools beginning to implement the AIW framework commit to the following 10 components for effective professional development, several of which are further explained later in this chapter and in Chapter 7:

## Key Components

1. *Team membership.* Teachers who volunteer to be on the pilot team represent at least two departments or grade levels and agree to participate on AIW teams comprising four to six members. When cross-grade or interdisciplinary teams are formed, they should involve all participants and not be divided into smaller groups of subject matter or grade-level specialists.

2. *Initial learning.* AIW team members (including the principal) participate in an AIW Kick-Off Institute that is scheduled before or early in the school year. The Kick-Off Institute should be two full days, preferably back to back to provide a detailed introduction to the AIW framework and research base and establish team norms and the schedule for meetings. Participants prepare for the institute by reading parts of this book and the Scoring Guide, and during the institute they use AIW standards and criteria to score, discuss, and give feedback on tasks, instruction, and student work, as they will throughout the year.

3. *AIW team scoring and discussion.* AIW team members agree to share, score, and give and receive feedback on artifacts of instruction, tasks/assignments, and student work from their own classes *that could be improved.* Lessons and tasks that score low because they are designed for basic knowledge and skills, such as a spelling test, should not be the focus of AIW team scoring. Rather, in the spirit of enhancing instructional practices, each teacher should determine what artifacts to bring to the team for which one or more of the AIW criteria can be improved. Critically sharing one's work and artifacts that the teacher wants to improve distinguishes AIW collaboration from most teachers' teaming experiences, which more typically focus on discussing students, curriculum, or data—not how to improve each individual teacher's practice.

4. *Job embedded.* Each AIW team meets for 4 to 6 hours each month of the school year to score, discuss, and offer suggestions for improvement of a lesson, assignment, or piece of student work, ideally with a job-embedded professional learning structure. This dedicated time for collaborative teacher learning might be accomplished through weekly common planning time for at least 1 hour, late starts or early release for at least 2 hours every other week, substitute teachers who release teachers for AIW team meetings on a regular basis, or additional

paid time for teachers before or after school. Most AIW schools use a combi-
nation of these approaches, and there is no one best way. But the 4 to 6 hours
per month is necessary to support sustained learning, generate momentum and
commitment, and improve practice.

5. *Ongoing learning.* Team meetings are organized so that during the year, each
participating teacher will have shared at least one lesson, assignment, and student work sample for team scoring and discussion using the criteria. This experience with all three types of artifacts encourages a deeper understanding of the
framework among the pilot teachers, which, in turn, will help them facilitate
teams of new AIW teachers as the initiative expands at the school in subsequent
years. It also prepares teachers for deliberation on conceptual-based instruction
and interdisciplinary or problem-based unit planning.

6. *AIW leadership team.* An AIW school leadership team composed of both teachers and administrators meets regularly to discuss implementation issues and
to score artifacts in order to enhance collective understanding of and commitment to the framework. Members of the leadership team who participate in
Center for AIW summer institutes continue to build local capacity for successful expansion beyond initial pilot teams.

7. *AIW coaching.* AIW lead coaches visit the school at least three times a year to
participate in team meetings and offer guidance and feedback to individual
teachers, teams, and administrators. As both an instructional coach and critical
friend, the AIW lead coach supports teams of teachers in their learning, provides expertise and course corrections for implementing the AIW framework
and professional development processes, and shares feedback with the leadership
team. While teams are encouraged to build their own shared understanding of
the AIW criteria, their scoring process must remain consistent with the spirit of
the published criteria that research has shown to contribute to higher and more
equitable student learning outcomes. The lead coach plays a key role in this.

8. *Administrator participation.* Administrators must learn the AIW framework,
participate as a learner in AIW professional development, and support teachers'
learning and efforts to improve their instruction. We explain key points later in
this chapter. The school administrator actively participates in the AIW Kick-
Off Institute, AIW team meetings, lead coaches' site visits, leadership team
meetings, and other important AIW school-based meetings.

9. *Scoring instruction.* During the year, AIW team members have the opportunity
to observe, score, and discuss a colleague's lesson in person or via video. If
teachers are initially hesitant or the school doesn't have appropriate equipment,
videos of web-based lessons outside the school could be used in the interim.

Observed lessons would be scored and discussed further in the next team meeting. Over the course of the year, each team member should strive to have at least one lesson scored and discussed by his or her team. It is not uncommon for some teachers to delay scoring instruction until, through observation of others, they become comfortable with the process. Still, each teacher in a team must eventually bring all three kinds of artifacts (tasks, student work, and instruction) to her or his AIW team to score.

10. *Plans to move forward.* Toward the end of the first or second year, teacher teams, in conjunction with the school leadership team, make plans for future years. These plans should address questions such as the following:

   • *Team structures and practices.* How will instruction and teacher collaboration time be scheduled so teachers can meet regularly to score? How often will teachers score lessons, tasks, and student work? How often will teachers share revised lessons and tasks to show increased expectations for Authentic Intellectual Work?

   • *Changing instruction.* Drawing on the scoring and discussion in their teams, when will teachers fine-tune, revise, or overhaul instruction, assignments, and assessments to better foster authentic work from students? How often will teachers try to teach lessons and assign tasks that scored at highest levels on AIW standards? What curriculum content best serves the rigorous intellectual demands of AIW?

   • *Project development:* How will leaders orient colleagues and teachers who are new to AIW or the school? How many new AIW teams should be formed, with how many teachers? Which pilot teachers will facilitate new teams and take on AIW coaching responsibilities at the school (as explained in Chapter 7)? What levels of administrative support will be required to succeed with the plans? This could involve structuring team and individual planning time, providing access to curriculum resources and coaching, assisting in the collection and analysis of relevant data, and gaining school board and parental/community support.

   • *Sustainability and coherence:* How will central office staff and the school board deal with administrative turnover? Identifying administrators who either have direct experience with AIW or are willing to sustain the effort is critical when hiring key positions such as principals, superintendents, and curriculum and professional development directors. Should AIW scores on student work be incorporated into student grades, and if so, how will this be explained to students and parents? How will leadership integrate required district or state mandates with AIW work or prevent them from distracting teachers from their AIW learning and implementation?

Making plans to address all these questions can be daunting, but since the questions specify incremental steps likely to maximize teacher buy-in, plans to address them deliberately will help build capacity to expand and sustain the work beyond the initial team of teachers.

We synthesize important components for AIW professional development in teams in Figure 6.1.

## SUPPORT FOR SCHOOL TEAMS

We emphasize three main sources of support for school teams in the early stages of the project: fellow teachers, school administrators, and AIW coaches. After AIW has been established, the sources of support expand to include the school board, students and parents, and ideally community organizations that partner on student projects that aim for more value beyond school. We discuss the important roles of teachers and school administrators next and address coaching in Chapter 7. In addition, this book's companion volume, *Schools and Districts Meeting Rigorous Standards Through Authentic Intellectual Work* (King, in press), features chapters from different schools about AIW professional learning.

## Teachers

From initial orientation through all phases of AIW implementation, individual teachers' success with AIW and that of the school as a whole depend on teachers collaborating with and supporting one another in the difficult intellectual work

**Figure 6.1  Load-Bearing Components of AIW Teams' Professional Development**

| Components | Contributes to . . . |
|---|---|
| AIW learning teams include four to six interdisciplinary or cross-grade teachers. Initial team members volunteer and participate in Kick-Off Institutes. | • Common understanding of shared framework and language |
| AIW learning teams meet 4 to 6 hours per month. AIW is job-embedded, not an add-on, as an essential part of professional development. | • Consistent and reliable AIW scoring |
| AIW learning team members bring artifacts (tasks, instruction, student work) that need improvement. Every team meeting includes scoring and feedback on teacher tasks or instruction and student work. | • Increased trust and stronger collaboration. |
| Building administrators participate as learners on a team and have AIW leadership meetings to build internal capacity and plan for expansion and sustainability. | • Improved teaching and assessment practices |
| AIW learning teams use AIW tools, including a scoring criteria booklet and rules of thumb, norms, and descriptive language. | • Increased student engagement and test scores |
| The school's AIW lead coach participates in team meetings and offers guidance and feedback to individual teachers, teams, and administrators. | • System-wide instructional coherence |

that AIW demands. AIW team meetings are the foundation of AIW professional development. Since the meetings require teachers to submit their artifacts (instruction, assignments, and student work) to colleagues for critical analysis, the work requires a level of honesty and risk-taking that can be productive only with trust and collegial support. Initial evaluations of Iowa's AIW reform revealed that teachers who experienced this process found it to be some of the most useful professional development they have had or could imagine experiencing, precisely because of the help that teachers offered one another. Emily's example highlights this benefit of AIW PD.

## Perspective From Practice

Emily Kobliska, Elementary Art Teacher, Gilbert, IA

*I see my students for a very limited amount of time each week and often struggle with managing instruction and student work time. I am always searching for ways to efficiently and effectively introduce students to new units and review without taking away too much of their production time. I sometimes fall into the trap of "telling" students what they need to know and asking simple recall questions to review quickly, without allowing them to uncover the learning themselves. After having my Picasso unit scored, I gained helpful insight into ways that I can challenge students to think deeper without sacrificing their art-making time. I really wasn't aware of the way I was posing my review questions to students until I saw myself on video — and then it was quite obvious! Having my instruction scored proved to be very beneficial to me as a teacher.*

## School Administrators

Principals have great influence on the success of any reform initiative. No school should undertake the AIW process unless at least one building administrator, preferably the principal, is actively involved from the outset. In the early stages, AIW teams should have school administrators as members who agree to help introduce AIW to teachers. As administrators participate in team activities, their role is to be a learner, leader, and advocate. These roles may be awkward for some administrators at first, but teachers can help integrate administrators as trusted team members by welcoming them as learners and holding them accountable for team norms, just as they would for other team members.

### Learners

School administrators' first responsibility is to learn, in teams, how to score and improve artifacts, because this is the foundation for understanding the nature and power of teaching according to the AIW framework. A couple of problems, however, often reduce administrator participation in this experience. One is the assumption that if administrators are not teaching, they have no artifact to bring to the team for analysis.

Though they may not have examples of lessons or tasks for students, or samples of student work, non-teachers can bring other useful artifacts; for example, an activity planned for staff professional development can be the "lesson" and the corresponding student work can be what the teachers "produce" in that session.

Another problem is how administrators fulfill their roles as instructional leaders, managers, and supervisors. Some have the tendency to act as managers, especially in schools where they move from team to team, assuming their job is to supervise or coordinate by rotating among teams. They may assume they can contribute more by observing how the program unfolds across the staff rather than by participating as a productive team member on one team. But those who stay in the role of supervisor lose sight of how AIW teaming differs from other professional development. For example, they may only criticize teachers' assignments, forgetting that the intended focus of the meeting is how to improve them; or they may believe they are familiar enough with their teachers' pedagogy, forgetting that the AIW teaming process is designed to promote pedagogical growth among its members and that all teachers can improve their teaching through active participation over time. Observing only snippets of conversations and snapshots of team discussions cannot reveal how pedagogy among team members evolves through AIW professional development.

The advantage of administrators scoring in a team is not simply an increase of their competence with the AIW framework so they understand what teachers are doing. Administrators who participate fully in team scoring meetings also report the following benefits:

- Collective trust increases as the team works together over time. As teachers take risks in sharing critiques of their work, administrators see them showing creative, critical thinking and constructive ways to help one another that otherwise would not be observed. And as one teacher said, "It doesn't take long to lose trust" when the principal isn't able to attend or chooses not to make AIW meetings a priority and doesn't attend.

- As the administrators' evaluator role recedes, they reconnect with personal roots in teaching and the joy of gaining new insights.

- Teachers on the team begin to see administrators in new ways, no longer as their boss but instead as a fellow educator experiencing the effort and joy of challenging intellectual work. Observing administrators in this role helps to enhance trust within the school.

Because such benefits occur only when the administrator shows up to the same team consistently, participates in scoring, and stays for the full meeting, we strongly recommend that school administrators (head and assistant principals) participate with teachers as members of at least one AIW team in as many of the activities as possible. In cases where districts have multiple schools involved in AIW, district curriculum directors might participate; in smaller districts (such as those with only one or a few schools), superintendents could elect to join a team as a learner. Superintendent Tim Lutz, a local coach in a rural district in northern Minnesota, shares his early impressions of being an AIW team member with the pilot team.

---

## Perspective From Practice

Tim Lutz, Superintendent and AIW Local Coach, Kelliher, MN

*As I moved forward with fully engaged participation in AIW, I found that my scoring ability improved whether scoring others' tasks, student work, or instruction or my own. During the course of this year, I believe I missed only one team meeting, and that was because I was out of town for a meeting I couldn't avoid. I made a conscious effort to attend every AIW team meeting, and that has paid off in numerous dividends, from improving my scoring ability to gaining the trust of my team members.*

*In giving up some "control" of my team and letting others facilitate, I was worried about losing control of how my team members would operate. I worried that two scenarios might play out: that team members would grandstand by showing off their strongest material or that team members would fly by the seat of their pants and begin presenting material that they put together at the last minute or materials that were nothing more than worksheets.*

*I need not have worried. From the beginning, the trust level on my team was such that teachers brought material that they truly felt needed improvement. That particular concern never materialized. However, on a couple of occasions, a team member would show up with what appeared to be a canned lesson plan (from a publisher) or a worksheet that was not appropriate for a scoring session. During those times, I kept myself from making any comments. However, on both occasions either the facilitator or another team member reminded the presenter that such material was not appropriate for the team to score. The situation was remedied in a truly authentic, collective, and organic fashion!*

*I feel that if I had pushed the issue, I would have been perceived as putting my administrator hat on and might have been given some push-back by one or more team members. By letting the team take care of the situation, we all grew collectively and in a way that was organic or specific to our own team. Indeed, our learning as a collective and as individuals was authentic—we created our own knowledge and created a meaningful solution to a problem that was specific to our team.*

---

### Leader and Advocate

As administrators come to understand the AIW process by actively participating on a team, the need for leadership in specific areas unique to the school situation becomes clearer. Regardless of the specific administrative tasks that emerge, administrators must lead in ways consistent with the principles of AIW implementation described earlier. To support AIW implementation, we have found administrative leadership and advocacy is critical in areas such as the following:

- Scheduling Kick-Off Institutes, team meetings, teacher planning time, in-service opportunities, and orientation of new teachers
- Assisting teachers in obtaining curriculum and assessment materials, and technology needed to teach according to the AIW framework

- Buffering teachers from demands (in curriculum, testing, other professional development initiatives) that interfere with teachers' efforts to implement AIW

- Securing funding—by allocating funds from the current budget and seeking additional support from the district or other sources—to support teachers' participation; the amount of funding needed will vary, depending on local circumstance

- Serving as a diplomat to explain the AIW reform to external parties, such as parents and school board members, or district, regional, and state officials, whose support may be necessary for the project to thrive

- Committing to at least 3 to 5 years of AIW development; instructional improvement is challenging work and AIW is not a quick fix, so AIW PD must be sustained over multiple years, and expansion within a building to all teachers must be carried out with adequate support

## GUIDING PRINCIPLES OF AIW IMPLEMENTATION

To help teachers and administrators with AIW PD, we emphasize four principles that maximize levels of success in teaching for Authentic Intellectual Work. Developed initially as a reflection tool (Carmichael, Martens, Zirps, Wahlert, & Peterson, 2013) for a lead coach's school site visit, these principles define a philosophy that AIW teachers experience through activities at the Kick-Off Institute, during site visits, and in regular team meetings. AIW leadership should use the guiding principles to help teams implement the load-bearing components described in Figure 6.1 and make decisions about participation in related projects or learning opportunities.

## 1. The Power of Being Authentic: Professional learning itself should reflect AIW

As teachers and administrators work to understand and implement AIW, they construct their own knowledge to reach in-depth understanding of how the standards might improve their practice rather than simply complying with or memorizing AIW standards. When professional development embodies AIW, participating teachers create meaningful solutions to the real problems of instruction, assessment, curriculum selection, and student evaluation that they face. Key questions stimulate professional learning that reflect AIW:

*Construction of knowledge.* Are we asking teachers to engage actively in higher order thinking to reach their own conclusions?

*Disciplined inquiry.* What concepts, problems, or processes related to the AIW framework are pursued in depth so that teachers can explain their conclusions through elaborated communication, rather than simply assigning scores?

*Value beyond school.* Will the results of professional discussion have meaningful payoff in teachers' practices after the team meeting or other related professional development activity?

## 2. The Power of the Collective: AIW professional learning should build a strong learning community

As discussed previously, teacher learning is best done in teams. While individual growth is important, its impact is greatest on students when a larger entity, such as a group of teachers, leadership team, coaching cohort, or region of the state collaborates on the effort. If individual or group decisions about teaching practice have been influenced by Authentic Intellectual Work in a team or group, they are likely to be more effective and defensible.

## 3. The Power of Being Organic: AIW implementation should vary with context

Different teachers, teams, schools, and districts will take different paths toward AIW implementation. Though all must share a focus on the AIW framework, our professional development supports each individual, each team, and each school in charting its distinct path to higher levels of the AIW standards. Without compromising the fidelity of the AIW framework, teachers, teams, and schools must be supported in charting their own way. Without that level of autonomy, the hard work and buy-in that AIW success requires will not emerge.

Consistent with organic implementation, success in teaching for AIW depends initially on voluntary participation by teachers and administrators who, after being well informed of AIW's potential, choose to work with it further. We have found that expansion beyond initial volunteers is best pursued through word of mouth from educators who have observed its actual success with students and teachers. After a successful pilot year, teachers and administrators who believe in the framework's value may put informal pressure on doubtful colleagues to become involved, which can eventually lead to more enthusiastic buy-in. In schools where a critical mass of the faculty have built competence and commitment to the AIW framework and want to expand schoolwide but some colleagues resist, it may be appropriate to require participation of additional faculty who would otherwise choose not to participate.

The goal of schoolwide instructional coherence focused on a powerful, research-based framework for intellectual rigor requires at some point a balance between volunteer staff commitment and staff participation required by the administration. While a voluntary approach may be sufficient in some settings, in more challenging settings with significant staff discord, it may be appropriate for administrators to require some teachers to participate in AIW teams for a reasonable trial period, as long as the teams are given sufficient support to maximize success. Without sufficient support, however, mandating

AIW professional development leads only to superficial, go-through-the-motions behavior that not only fails to improve teaching but also generates teacher opposition to AIW and required professional development in general.

## 4. The Power of Risk-Taking:
## Taking intellectual and professional risks should be supported

Since AIW professional development emphasizes sharing, scoring and defending scores, and providing feedback on teachers' lessons, assignments, and student work, it requires that teachers constantly subject their professional work to the critiques of colleagues. This entails taking a risk in a "public" setting that an individual's or a team's work will be scored low or considered in need of improvement. During professional development activities, teacher leaders and administrators must support risk-taking in the school culture and build teams where individuals work hard to help one another and the group as a whole and respect unique paths that individuals and teams may take.

A teacher's willingness to entertain critiques and suggestions about his or her work must be seen not as subjecting oneself to colleagues' judgment of professional competence but as opportunities for help. Conversely, those who offer critique and suggestions must learn to do so in ways that can improve lessons, tasks, and evaluation of student work and understanding of the AIW framework, rather than offering only summary judgments or subjective commentary.

Three guidelines that build trust and promote risk taking during scoring sessions are (1) using descriptive, not evaluative, language; (2) supporting a score with specific evidence from the artifact rather than one's own personal experiences; and (3) connecting that evidence to specific rubric language for the particular AIW standard being discussed. The analysis of artifacts in Part II illustrates the use of these guidelines when scoring.

### CONCLUSION

The substantive focus for professional development is the AIW framework for rigorous teaching and learning that increases student effort and engagement, and promotes higher and more equitable levels of achievement. This chapter's approaches and guiding principles align with research on best practice in professional development (e.g., Elmore, 2002; King & Bouchard, 2011; Lieberman & Miller, 2007). Effective professional development

- is sustained and focused;

- involves leaders and teachers collaborating in active learning, inquiry, and reflective dialogue;

- addresses knowledge and skills related to curriculum, instruction, and assessment; and

- relates to key contextual factors of a particular school.

Teachers and school teams who choose to embark on the journey toward Authentic Intellectual Work can use this chapter for ongoing discussion. Though we have offered evidence-based sources and reasoned argument, successful implementation of the AIW framework ultimately depends on educators internalizing its value through their own practice, critical inquiry, and discussion. Teacher Laura Hensley sums up its impact.

## Perspective From Practice

Laura Hensley, West Sioux High School, West Sioux, IA

*I have been an educator for over a decade in two states, three high schools, and two middle schools. I have gone through various staff developments and multiple districtwide curriculum investments. With all investments, school districts are looking for returns like gains in student achievement and staff collaboration. Yet most of the investments I have been a part of as an educator never produce returns or results that are measurable or have longevity. I was a part of a PLC [professional learning community] in Oregon. . . . We would get together, but have no direction, and we would end up just complaining. It was more damaging than productive.*

*Then last year (2012) I was introduced to the AIW framework and I felt as if a switch had been turned on. When our AIW groups meet (with a few exceptions; nothing is 100% perfect) there are no staged leaders. It is a shared experience and thus a universally invested experience. WOW . . . AIW says come on into the discussion, see what you think, you are considered an equal, and your opinion matters. Take your time and focus on what areas you need help with. There is no pressure on a few to lead in a top-down approach. AIW hands down is the most influential and positive professional development experience I have ever been a part of. AIW has been the most profound and important professional development I have ever done. For over a decade I have felt frustrated when collaborating with my peers and isolated in my desire to think outside the box. Yet the "go it alone" philosophy never helped me produce the results in the classroom I desired.*

*Now I realize it was because my collaboration time lacked a common language, objective, and purpose. When I sit with my AIW colleagues and score a task, student work, or instruction, I'm empowered by teachers leading teachers. Together we break down the barriers of isolation and help each other become better professionals in the classroom by creating student work that is meaningful and purposeful. I hear feedback that is productive and constructive without being critical or evaluative of my personal attributes. An AIW team meeting provides a safe and supportive collaborative atmosphere for teachers because it keeps you grounded in a common purpose, developing authentic intellectual student work. AIW builds on your strengths while still exposing areas of improvement and helping you utilize that total experience to produce quality student work.*

# Chapter 7
## External Support

*Building Capacity for Improved Teaching in Schools*

### OVERVIEW

Any reform to improve classroom instruction must address the problem of building and sustaining human capacity. This entails building the competence and motivation of educators, both individually and collectively, by providing professional development and the material resources and organizational structures to implement the reform. Chapter 6 described how Authentic Intellectual Work (AIW) professional development builds capacity in individual schools through formation of teacher teams, orientation kick-offs, team scoring of artifacts, and continuous coaching on site. Based on lessons learned in the Center for AIW's partnerships with school districts, the first half of this chapter responds to analogous questions from district leaders considering whether to invest in AIW reform.

The second half of the chapter addresses the problem of sustaining initial efforts in schools and expanding to more teachers and schools. While local leadership is critical to building AIW capacity within a school, school leaders cannot do it alone. Even the most skilled, passionate leaders depend on cooperation and, in many cases, assistance from the district, state, and other external organizations that typically offer or fund professional development and sustain reform efforts over time. While the Center's experience is unique, research over many years (e.g., Honig, 2008; Slavin, 1998; Weick, 1976) shows how different instructional reforms live or die, based on the kind of support (or lack thereof) they get from external agencies such as districts, regional service agencies, state departments of education, universities, and other organizations, such as the Center for AIW, that work to improve instruction.

### LESSONS LEARNED AND RECOMMENDATIONS—IS AIW FOR YOUR DISTRICT?

As news of AIW success spread, district leaders considered whether AIW reform could benefit their students. Some had already built a collaborative reflective culture and hoped to deepen it. Others were interested in using AIW criteria to develop a common intellectual mission to improve student learning. Still other administrators wanted to pursue almost any initiative likely to raise test scores. Below we respond to a number of questions raised by districts in considering whether and to what extent to invest in AIW professional development.

## Since AIW reform seems so powerful, how can we implement it districtwide as soon as possible?

While immediate, large-scale reform often sounds appealing, the AIW initiative should not be implemented too broadly or quickly. Promising research-based reforms have too often been prematurely expanded before initial adopters have built the capacity to sustain them. While an "all-in" start can appear to strengthen a district's collective vision, it is always precarious. AIW requires starting small because its success depends on complex intellectual work and teamwork that is best fostered with small numbers of teachers and teams in a pilot effort. Districts or schools that choose to adopt the program for everyone at once never develop enough capacity on a small scale to show the success necessary to justify further expansion.

The second reason it's important to start small is to capitalize on the organic nature of the AIW professional development. Individual teachers, pilot teams, and buildings will all engage in the process differently, which is essential for letting the experience deepen enough to transfer into the classroom. Pilot teams are usually very insightful in determining the pacing for AIW expansion, and this builds faculty buy-in. Finally, as pilot teachers take time to gain experience, they can later become effective local AIW coaches.

- The closest example of successful initial districtwide implementation was a district that had a pilot team doing so well in one elementary school that the superintendent required all the other schools to start AIW the following year. Luckily, he put in place the necessary resources to support implementation and sent leadership to a summer institute. This example of quick expansion is an exception to the rule. AIW has always been best implemented as a limited pilot before full staff or full district implementation.

**Recommendation**: To maximize later success, start with one to two pilot teams per school. It is not necessary to have every school involved in AIW, but if AIW seems consistent with other district programs, districts might start with up to two pilot teams in multiple schools as long as pilot teams help determine schools' future involvement rather than central office or administration dictating it.

## How successful have districts been at funding AIW through existing funding streams?

Because AIW teams must focus entirely on AIW analysis and building the culture it requires, their AIW work should not be seen as fulfilling any other separately funded program, such as implementing new curriculum, teacher evaluation, or categorically mandated programs to serve defined groups of students. Including AIW work under such funding streams is likely to distract teachers from the work of AIW. One possible exception is funding for professional learning communities, because goals in these programs are typically consistent with the teaming and collaborative reflection required in AIW professional development.

- One district used an existing leadership grant to offset its AIW costs; unfortunately, teachers who had been designated as "teacher leaders" saw their role as "leader" as synonymous with expert, or trainer, which prevented them from subjecting their own low-scoring artifacts to analysis by their colleagues. The AIW leadership team eventually became aware of the problem, but could not reframe the role of teacher leaders from being a "master teacher" to being a "master learner." Ultimately, AIW was not sustained in this district.

- In a different district, a leadership grant promoted teacher choice by allowing different reforms to happen simultaneously in a school. The administrator hoped all teachers would rotate through each initiative. Because AIW was one of several choices for teachers, only those interested in making major changes to their classroom practices signed up. The principal admitted in retrospect that the very teachers who might have benefitted most from AIW chose a funded program that had lower expectations for classroom application. Furthermore, those who had started with AIW did not want to stop scoring artifacts with their AIW teams in order to participate in a different initiative. Since AIW teams had more immediate positive impact on students, only students in those classrooms benefited.

**Recommendation**: Whenever possible, AIW funding, which we discuss in more detail later, should be included in a grant for that purpose, not funded through an external stream with a possibly distracting focus. This helps both the funders and participants to be accountable to each other. Teacher leadership grants can help to fund local coaches or sustain AIW after it has been well established in selected teams and schools. Although AIW can be consistent with other initiatives, administrators must protect the pilot teams' experience so teachers can concentrate on functioning well with their initial teams before they are expected to lead AIW in other contexts.

## AIW seems worth pursuing, but our district prefers to let teachers and administrators implement it in their own ways.

Enthusiasm for AIW has been spread by word of mouth in some districts, and teachers may claim they have read the material and are using it to guide their instruction. However, if research-based reforms are implemented only through general knowledge, without careful attention to subtle details and distinctions in the original work, they cannot be expected to replicate the research-based results. If a district decides to make

AIW a professional development focus, central office staff developers and administrators should be involved from the start in AIW orientation sessions. Waiting until teachers and principals have tried it on their own can create problems over time. When central office administrators join AIW late, there is always the risk that they will try to re-introduce the very culture that teachers and principals may have been dislodging, turning the decision-making process into a school versus district power struggle.

- One district, with varying degrees of success across schools, decided to create its own AIW process. District leaders rewrote all the AIW scoring criteria by combining AIW language with that of another instructional reform program. District leaders then required the schools to use the district version. The mandate applied to the most successful AIW school, which had made substantial gains in student achievement, despite protest against the changed scoring criteria from the principal and staff. Unfortunately, by the time the district office withdrew its demand, enthusiasm for AIW in the school had lost momentum. The trailblazing principal who had started the work had retired. Even though the district had invested in local coaches, the struggle left no one with enough AIW experience and leadership or power to sustain early successes and the local capacity that successful schools had built.

**Recommendation**: Districts that choose AIW reform must implement the reform according to key components outlined in Chapter 6. If there is the possibility of expanding AIW districtwide, central office administrators should join school-based pilot teams from the start to better understand the framework and the professional development process. Early and continuing involvement by district staff helps to sustain initial teams and also better positions district staff to lead expansion when appropriate.

## We have a large district with more than 20,000 students. How can the Center help districts build their own capacity to implement AIW teaching in their schools?

Even in large districts AIW reform must start small, beginning with pilot teams that follow the key components outlined in Chapter 6. But by including staff from the district central office who provide professional development to multiple schools on AIW pilot teams, districts begin the process of developing their own cadre of lead and local coaches. The same approach can be used to develop capacity at the regional or state level.

- The best example is the Center's collaboration with the Iowa Department of Education. In 2007, the AIW Iowa project started at nine pilot schools of various sizes. Each school had pilot teams coached by two Center coaches. Since one of the Department's goals was to build Iowa's capacity to bring on more AIW schools, it funded costs to certify coaches at the local, regional, and state levels from 2008–2009 until 2014. Because of this investment, many districts in

Iowa have the leadership and coaching capacity to manage increasing demand for AIW. This is best illustrated in Figure 7.1 in the following section, AIW Coaching in AIW Professional Development, which illustrates a gradual increase in local coaches and a decrease in external coaches provided by the Center or other external organizations.

As illustrated in the following example, a large district can minimize future dependence on external coaches by developing its own coaches. Imagine the district's leadership hopes to eventually offer AIW professional development to any of its schools interested in AIW. First, leadership would assign three central office staff who are responsible for staff development to work as AIW liaisons (described in the next section) with the external lead coach at each of three initial pilot schools. After one year of studying with the lead coach in the role of AIW liaison, they become eligible to participate in the AIW coaching residency, which requires they coach their own pilot teams in new AIW schools. The external lead coach would continue during the second year helping the three original pilot schools expand according to their readiness and providing the district coaches-in-residence with additional experience in building capacity. If three district staff developers moved from AIW liaisons to coaches-in-residence and finally became certified coaches, the district would have enough AIW coaches to grow from three pilot schools in the first year to as many as nine schools the second year. And it would now have certified AIW coaches on its own staff to accommodate future schools interested in starting AIW.

**Recommendation**: Large districts (or regions) that anticipate including multiple schools in AIW professional development should build in participation from the central office early to increase the district's capacity to assist its schools. Early coordination enables district personnel to become active participants in districtwide implementation, which reduces costs for sustaining the work over the long term. While the Center's experience with Iowa is unique, other states with inter-district providers like Iowa's Area Education Agencies (AEAs) can invest in preparing coaches for districts interested in implementing AIW professional development. External help from sources like this can help districts build their own capacity.

## AIW COACHING IN AIW PROFESSIONAL DEVELOPMENT

AIW lead and local coaches build capacity for well-paced and well-supported AIW expansion. The primary role of lead coaches is to start AIW at a new school or district until it decides to invest in preparing its own coaches. Both lead and local coaches are critical for early success and long-term sustainability of AIW teaching. This section describes the origin of AIW coaching, how coaches work with teachers and teams, and parts of their professional learning that distinguishes AIW coaching from other approaches to coaching.

## Origins of AIW Coaching

The first AIW lead coaches-in-residency experience began in 2008–2009, and over the next 6 years, 39 lead coaches from the Iowa Department of Education and AEAs and 155 local coaches from AIW schools and districts supported professional development with the AIW framework. In partnership with the Iowa Department of Education (which supplied most of the funding during early years of implementation) and working also with some of the state's AEAs, the Center for AIW developed the approach to prepare lead coaches described below.

Aspiring lead coaches prepare for the residency by serving as liaisons to experienced lead coaches in two or more schools for at least one year. As liaisons, they learn more about the AIW rationale and research, score with AIW teams, and participate in site visits with the lead coach. Many liaisons found they had to "unlearn" or abandon traditional roles of a consultant or PD provider as trainer or expert, that is, to put less emphasis on providing information and giving "right" answers and more on helping to facilitate a team of teachers learning together and from one another how to apply the AIW framework for teaching and learning.

With increasing numbers of schools in Iowa to serve, lead coaches would work with the newer schools and reduce their coaching in schools that had been involved with AIW for several years. To help continue capacity building at the school and district levels, the Center developed the AIW local coaches-in-residency experience. The local coaches-in-residency program prepares teachers or administrators to work with lead coaches until the local coaches can become responsible for maintaining and sustaining AIW in their own schools and districts.

As shown in Figure 7.1, the percentage of Center AIW coaches coaching Iowa schools, funded by the Department of Education, decreased from 100% in 2007 to less than 1% in 2014, while the percentage of local coaches from schools and districts increased from 0% to over 80% (Carmichael & Martens, in press). Furthermore, by investing in lead coach development with its own staff (shown in gray) and with those AEAs interested in AIW (shown in stripes), Iowa has over 30 lead coaches to support future schools in starting AIW professional development.

## The Responsibilities of Lead and Local Coaches

Both lead and local coaches are critical to sustaining AIW instruction and keeping professional development for it on track. How to teach so that students advance in producing Authentic Intellectual Work cannot be summarized into a set of skills and knowledge that can be given to a teacher in a day or two of training. It requires a way of thinking and teaching that develops over time. Supporting that development—by facilitating collective scoring, discussion, and feedback on instruction, assignments and tasks and student work, and by offering course corrections for the AIW teams—is the AIW (lead or local) coach's primary role.

Figure 7.1 Comparison of AIW Coaches in Iowa by Organization and Percentage, 2007–2015

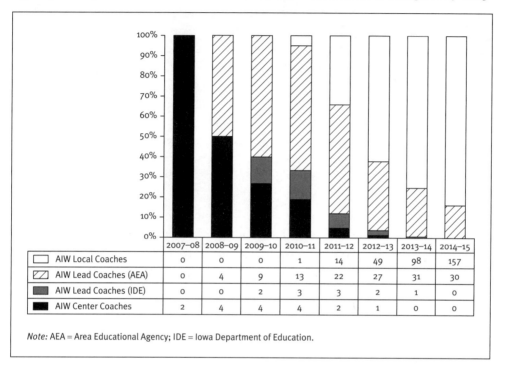

| | 2007–08 | 2008–09 | 2009–10 | 2010–11 | 2011–12 | 2012–13 | 2013–14 | 2014–15 |
|---|---|---|---|---|---|---|---|---|
| ☐ AIW Local Coaches | 0 | 0 | 0 | 1 | 14 | 49 | 98 | 157 |
| ▨ AIW Lead Coaches (AEA) | 0 | 4 | 9 | 13 | 22 | 27 | 31 | 30 |
| ▦ AIW Lead Coaches (IDE) | 0 | 0 | 2 | 3 | 3 | 2 | 1 | 0 |
| ■ AIW Center Coaches | 2 | 4 | 4 | 4 | 2 | 1 | 0 | 0 |

*Note:* AEA = Area Educational Agency; IDE = Iowa Department of Education.

The most successful coaches enter their cohort residencies with the following abilities, experiences and dispositions. These characteristics should be considered before a school or educational agency decides to invest in and select particular educators to become AIW coaches:

- ability to score tasks, student work, and instruction in most subjects according to AIW criteria

- interest in school-based professional development

- interest in open, honest personal reflection

- willingness to challenge others to improve professional practice

- at least one year of active, constructive participation on an AIW team, demonstrating reliability, openness, and ongoing interest in AIW

To be effective, coaches must think deeply about how team members experience the coaching sessions and how coaching and team meetings affect teachers' learning of the AIW framework, for better or worse. For professional developers accustomed to giving predetermined answers as experts or lead trainers, this approach requires "unlearning" the more common roles. Coaches-in-residence learn to create psychological space for teachers and administrators to take the intellectual risks of critical inquiry demanded by the AIW framework. In addition to understanding how authentic learning is defined by the AIW criteria and using the guiding principles to frame their coaching decisions, we use a tool called the AIW Coaching Diamond (Carmichael & Wahlert, 2014) shown in Figure 7.2 to help coaches reflect on how well they and others are doing in response to their coaching.

*AIW Learning.* This quadrant is the "what" of AIW coaching. It includes understanding AIW research and theory and how to accurately score artifacts by becoming fluent in the framework's scoring standards. The coach helps team members analyze the degree to which an actual lesson (not a lesson plan), assignment, or piece of student work shows evidence of (a) original application of knowledge and skills rather than just routine application of facts and procedures, (b) in-depth disciplined study of a particular topic or problem, and (c) a product or presentation that has meaning beyond success in school. Beyond scoring the quality of teachers' artifacts, the coach must help the team offer useful feedback to revise and improve them.

*Team Facilitation.* This part of the diamond is "how" to successfully engage the team. It emphasizes two elements: facilitating learning and facilitating logistics. To facilitate learning, coaches are taught early in their residency that AIW facilitation involves construing their work with teacher teams as a form of teaching that itself can be scored using criteria for authentic instruction. The more the coach structures the instruction (that is, the kind of facilitation offered during coaching) to score high, the more positive the learning within the team. Logistics include helping ensure the team adheres to

**Figure 7.2  AIW Coaching Diamond**

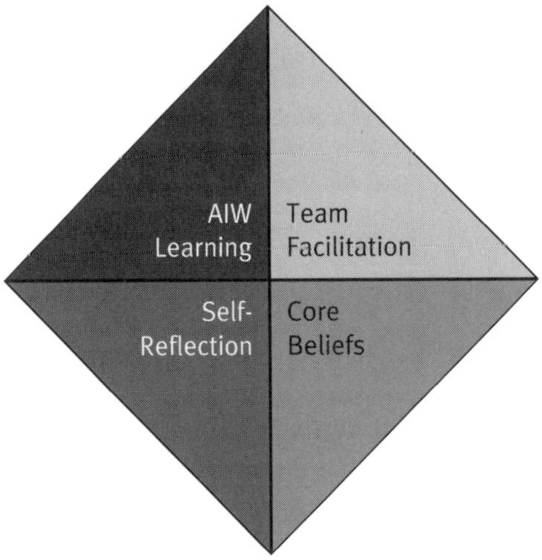

the key elements of AIW professional learning, described in Chapter 6 as load-bearing components. These include maintaining a team of four to six people that meet to score 4 to 6 hours per month, and keeping the team focused on AIW criteria, standards, and rubrics during the team meeting to score and improve artifacts. Coaches help teams hold to whatever norms and procedures they've established regarding the scheduling and conduct of the meetings, discussion etiquette, and the types of artifacts that teachers bring. Coaches who find themselves leading AIW learning in contexts other than teacher teams, such as staff professional development sessions or leadership team meetings, are most succeesful when their facilitation itself embodies Authentic Intellectual Work.

*Self-Reflection.* The self-reflection quadrant includes three forms of reflection. The individual level represents each team member being receptive to feedback and thoughtfully challenging one another's thinking. Self-reflection also occurs at the team level when all members help one another to be intellectually open to critical reflection and to constructively resolve disagreement while scoring or discussing other issues. The third form of reflection asks coaches to recognize how their personalities and facilitation styles affect others. Reflective coaches self-monitor how they influence the team, and they use strategies to reduce their unintended negative impact on team members. The point is to prevent coaches' personalities from controlling the team's experience in ways that may stifle the constructive intellectual inquiry required for successful AIW professional development.

*Core Beliefs.* The core beliefs quadrant refers to beliefs of the members (including the coach) and the overall tone or feeling of the team generated by the dispositions of its members. Coaches are expected to understand that educators hold different beliefs that influence their capacity to implement AIW and the quality of reflection within the team. Beliefs may differ on the nature and value of the AIW framework, how to teach their subjects, their colleagues' and their own teaching effectiveness, or their expectations of students. Coaches must be sensitive to how these beliefs affect work within the team and must respond to them in ways that build positive energy and commitment to teaching according to the AIW framework.

Each AIW team has a unique set of dispositions that influences the tone of its work. The most successful teams foster risk-taking, personal growth, constructive criticism, and healthy debate. But some teams are less disposed to learning. They can communicate negativity with unhelpful sidebar comments, entrenched thinking, or excessive controversy. It's also possible for teams to be too positive without enough disagreement, reinforcing an uncritical norm of groupthink that maintains the status quo. One of the responsibilities of coaches is to help teams constructively address how well the team members balance being supportive while still creating a climate that encourages differing viewpoints and constructive criticism. Of course, coaches have different comfort zones in dealing with these issues and must develop skills and dispositions that allow them to discuss issues of the team's climate with its members.

This quadrant also helps coaches understand how their core beliefs about a team can affect, for better or worse, individual team members' enthusiasm or the team's overall success in AIW professional development. Some coaches may express excessive intensity or expertise, overemphasizing procedures and "getting it right." Others can be quiet or passive coaches who reduce the team's energy. The most effective coaches show enthusiasm for the power of AIW and reinforce what Carol Dweck (2006) calls a *growth mindset*, that is, a strong belief that *all* team members can and will grow throughout the AIW inquiry process. Successful coaches communicate these beliefs, knowing that they motivate team members to take more risks, try new approaches, and use team resources to improve their teaching. Facing core beliefs constructively is a tall order that every coach has struggled with, but working explicitly with this quadrant in the diamond helps coaches improve their ability to positively affect a team's growth by believing in the potential success of both the team and each team member.

## Perspective From Practice

Pennie Rude, Teacher and AIW Local Coach, Kelliher Schools, Kelliher, MN

*I experienced a lot of growth in the team facilitation area, which really wasn't a shocker to me, especially considering my role of moving from the pilot team into more of a leadership role as a coach in training with peers who are all new to the AIW process. However, during this past year, I learned a lot about myself and how to become a more effective, efficient, personable, communicative, and reflective coach. I had to learn how to stand in the tragic gap and be okay with this process not only for my own personal growth but also for the growth of my team in the AIW journey. Since one of my strengths is being a fast thinker with the ability to quickly solve problems, I had to understand that my shadow side could take over. At any moment, I could quickly dominate the part of scoring where as a team we discuss ideas for changing what we are scoring. I really had to work on focusing on the process and organic nature of AIW to get to the solutions.*

*Being driven is also one of my strengths, which could quickly turn into a shadow side, especially when coaching and collaborating with a new AIW team. My get-it-done attitude could have easily pushed our scoring times to function like a military drill team rather than focusing on everyone understanding the nature of the process. One thing I did to help curb this shadow side was sit with my back to the clock and not worry about time and just focus on the process of scoring with my team. Team facilitation for me will be an ongoing process, where I need to effectively communicate and reflect to my team how my strengths as a leader can hijack our scoring process. Or how any one of our strengths as a team member can turn into a shadow side and derail our team cohesiveness.*

### SUSTAINING LOCAL CAPACITY

A district that commits to individual and collective learning in schools with central office support typically increases its capacity by developing its own coaches. Another critical step is to foster a regional professional community for implementing the AIW framework. Since every school's implementation varies based on context, AIW teachers, administrators, and coaches find great value in sustaining their growth by learning from one another. Without such nested communities of support, professional development for AIW may transform classroom practice within a school but is unlikely to sustain and expand these promising efforts.

Four key themes for expanding and sustaining capacity for AIW beyond initial pilots have emerged through our work in Iowa and in schools and districts in Connecticut, Georgia, Minnesota, and Wisconsin:

1. Starting small before expanding, as previously emphasized in the section "Lessons Learned—Is AIW for Your District?"

2. Developing AIW coaches, discussed in the previous section

3. Networking among AIW schools, described next

4. Understanding how external agents support local schools and districts to help wean them from major external support and to build program coherence that resists adoption of latest fads

## Networking Among AIW Schools

Just as pilot teams of teachers at a school generate momentum for building-wide implementation, a single school often prompts expansion to other schools in the district and eventually to a districtwide focus on Authentic Intellectual Work. District leadership commits to AIW professional development for multiple years, establishes a districtwide AIW leadership team, and supports staff members in becoming local coaches. Cross-school and district networking opportunities offer special expertise and collegial support for sustaining and expanding capacity to implement the AIW framework. In addition to school-based coaching, AIW lead coaches also facilitate regional collaboration and AIW networking. When local coaches emerge from different schools in a common region, the lead coaches work with local coaches to increase local capacity.

In Iowa, because of the Department of Education's initial investment in developing lead and local coaches, districts and AEAs later supported regional networking with minimal support from the Center for AIW. In Minnesota, the impetus to implement AIW came from districts in one part of the state, so local AIW coaches began working with Center lead coaches, planning eventually to establish regional lead coaches. Although contexts and sources of support differ, networks provide valuable opportunities to sustain and refresh AIW learning. Based on the Center's partnerships with local, regional, and state agencies, Figure 7.3 shows how AIW learning experiences can be supported through regional collaboration.

## An Example of Positive Impact From Regional Networking

In rural Minnesota, a consortium of districts formed to advance AIW implementation. Together with the Minnesota Rural Education Association (MREA), this voluntary association of rural school districts illustrates how word of mouth can disseminate

**Figure 7.3  AIW Learning and Networking Experiences, and Regional Collaboration**

| Learning Experiences | Opportunities for Regional Collaboration |
| --- | --- |
| Kick-Off Institutes<br><br>*Two days of initial training in the fall for new AIW teams conducted by certified AIW coaches and held at an AIW school.* | This experience is required for all new pilot teams. New AIW teams from different schools and districts may join the same kick-off. While regional collaboration is possible, it is not required. |
| Mid-year Institutes<br><br>*One or two days of mid-year regional collaboration for AIW teachers. Secondary teachers meet in groups of the discipline or subjects they teach, bringing artifacts to score. Elementary teachers typically meet in grade bands (K–2, 4–6, etc.). Common content background allows deeper conceptual scoring and analysis. Typically held in winter and coordinated by certified lead or local AIW coaches and held at an AIW school.* | Mid-year institutes promote networks designed for regional collaboration. The institutes further develop a common language and understanding for rigorous learning and facilitate an informal exchange of AIW assignments and curriculum. Successful mid-year institutes require regional collaboration among multiple AIW schools and districts. But large districts with more than 10,000 students and many AIW schools may have their own mid-year institutes. |
| AIW Coaches Development<br><br>*AIW coaching preparation, usually directed by the Center, includes extended learning over multiple days with people from varying sites. The experiences are facilitated by certified AIW coaches and held at a central location in the region. Other organizations may direct preparation of coaches, provided they do so with Center guidance and conduct the activities with trained AIW coaches.* | Both lead and local coach residencies include educators from multiple locations. This enhances regional coordination of mid-year institutes and joint kick-offs. Certified coaches are required to continue their AIW growth by collaborating with coaches outside their organization or school to problem solve, score, and continue advancing their learning with the Coaching Diamond. |
| Summer Coordinator and Next Steps Academies<br><br>*The AIW Coordinator Academy is a 3-day summer retreat for schools ready to expand AIW in one school or across a district. The Next Steps Academy extends and deepens implementation through specific tools for local program evaluation. Both are facilitated by certified AIW coaches.* | Coordinator and Next Steps Academies bring together staff from schools and districts at similar stages in AIW development. The academies are located only in areas with many schools at similar stages in AIW development, but the academies are open to all AIW schools in the United States with similar learning needs. |
| Extended opportunities for advanced AIW learning<br><br>*The Center develops AIW extended learning opportunities based on the learning needs of sites that have sustained AIW for multiple years. These are coordinated by the Center and facilitated by certified AIW coaches and currently held in regional locations.* | Any AIW teacher from any school who has had significant experience with AIW may enhance their application of the framework through data collection training or student professional development workshops, or by joining a unit planning or online learning cohort. Because every school has teachers with varying years of involvement, these experiences require regional collaboration to increase the quality of learning and offset costs. |

interest in AIW, even without state-level support. A reform-minded rural superintendent was attending a national conference and was struck by how enthusiastic Iowa superintendents were about AIW in their schools. Returning to Minnesota, he conferred with the executive director of MREA, an AIW lead coach. They invited four rural school districts, the Minnesota Northwest Service Cooperative, and two regional foundations into a collaborative effort to support five schools, each with large numbers of Native American students, to start and sustain AIW. Beginning in 2012, this effort continued through 2014–2015 with the districts providing two thirds of the funding for AIW lead coaches in the third year of the project.

## THE ROLE OF EXTERNAL AGENTS

While external support from the district and beyond can launch AIW professional development in a major way, successful implementation in the long term relies on the capacity of educators in their local schools and districts. Some schools need more external help for longer periods. Michael Fullan (2001) captured the tension when he argued, "The need for external intervention is inversely proportionate to how well the school is progressing. . . . In the long run, however, effectiveness depends on developing internal commitment in which ideas and internal motivation of the vast majority of organizational members become activated" (p. 46). No organization should ever consider that its learning is finished or that it is unable to benefit from continued coaching and other forms of external support.

This final section describes two areas of support that external agencies, from district to state, can offer to build AIW capacity for long-term implementation and sustainability: program coherence for AIW learning and funding. While funding is necessary and may seem most important, it's not sufficient. External agencies also need to support AIW schools through leadership that emphasizes program coherence for AIW learning.

### Program Coherence for AIW Learning

Long-standing challenges to successful instructional reform do not disappear with implementation of AIW. Changes in leadership, changes in state policy, and new funding incentives all create the risk that, instead of working to sustain and improve a promising initiative, a school or district will abandon it and instead chase after the latest fad. This leads to a plethora of unrelated initiatives, an incoherence in instructional programs that depresses student achievement and teacher morale. By offering an instructional framework that spans diverse grade levels and subjects, AIW provides program coherence. External agents who want to assist AIW can support it, not only by providing resources but also by establishing AIW as a solid priority and by resisting changes in leadership, policy, or funding incentives that can undermine its sustainability. Figure 7.4 summarizes how different agencies can support program coherence for AIW learning, which is critical to build and sustain capacity for AIW instruction. The figure also identifies problems that often arise from agencies' lack of or declining external support.

In Pike County, Georgia, a district of 3,500 students, 43% of them in poverty, AIW began in 2013–2014 with pilot teams and leaders across the district's four schools and from the central office who worked together, along with a Center coach. By scheduling about 7 hours of AIW PD per month (provided mainly through funding of substitutes and staff development days) and by supporting the learning of successive teams of teachers, the district made a sustained commitment of time and resources. According to the superintendent, Mike Duncan, in order to bring together their focus on 21st-century skills, core curriculum power standards, and performance assessments for units of study, teachers needed to improve their instruction. For Duncan, it's the district's job to

**Figure 7.4 External Agencies' Support for AIW Capacity and Problems They May Create**

| Agency | Type of Support* | Problems |
|--------|------------------|----------|
| State | Provides multi-year funding of AIW professional development<br><br>Coordinates statewide and cross-region institutes<br><br>Conducts project evaluations | Political support dwindles.<br><br>Financial and resource allocations are reduced.<br><br>There is uneven AIW capacity among different districts and regions. |
| Regional | Allocates staff time to become AIW lead coaches<br><br>Coordinates workshops and institutes for multiple schools | Initial support from schools, districts, and regional agencies ends prematurely.<br><br>Interested schools find no external support. |
| District | Commits to fund and help lead AIW PD for the long term<br><br>Funds and allocates staff time to develop AIW lead or local coaches at the district and school levels | Changes in leadership reduce or end AIW support in favor of other initiatives.<br><br>District leaders fail to prioritize instructional improvement. |

*These descriptions represent the Center's experience working with different agencies to date. But theoretically, the activities in each cell could be supported by district, regional, or state agencies and/or grants from other sources.

help teachers improve through ongoing learning opportunities centered on the common framework and language of AIW. To sustain and deepen this work, district resources will support local coach development in 2015–2016, with two coaches for each of the four schools and four coaches from the district office. The examples in Minnesota and Georgia show that districts can successfully sustain and expand AIW implementation, even in the absence of resources from the state or other external agencies.

Hopefully, external agencies help schools prioritize professional development for instructional improvement to strengthen instructional program coherence, that is, ensuring that instruction throughout the school is coordinated, aimed at clear learning goals, and sustained over time. Typically, though, student and staff learning is weakened by externally initiated programs that are discrete and unrelated, like ornaments on a Christmas tree, resulting in fragmented improvement initiatives that address only limited numbers of students and staff or are ended after short periods of time. Research (e.g., Childress, Elmore, Grossman, & Johnson, 2007; Newmann, Smith, Allensworth, & Bryk, 2001; Payne, 2008) clearly demonstrates the importance of program coherence for improving teaching quality and student achievement.

## Funding

Building school-level capacity to support expansion requires commitment of funds. For example, in Pike County, Georgia, funds came from school or district professional development budgets. In Minnesota, districts sought a foundation grant as seed money before committing to full implementation with district funds. And in Iowa, the AIW project received state funds to initiate significant AEA participation.

Ideally, from whatever source, funders should have a long-term plan that begins with pilot teams at pilot schools, that resists rapid expansion to new schools or districts until initial pilot sites have sufficient capacity to support modest expansion, and that commits to eventual expansion so that initial participants will belong to a larger supportive network. This pace is contrary to the more common tendency of showcasing a promising intervention by disseminating a one-size-fits-all model to many teachers and schools quickly. Ironically, expanding quickly often seems necessary to impress and gain support from external agents who prefer to have a "big impact," but premature expansion actually undermines building capacity.

Schools use funds to help defray costs for the following aspects of professional development:

- **Internal development** for AIW PD, such as offering stipends for initial teacher participation and paying for substitutes so that teachers and administrators can attend kick-offs, meet regularly in AIW teams, and purchase materials

- **Cross-school and district learning experiences** at regional AIW events such as the beginning-of-the-year Kick-Off Institutes, Mid-year Collaboration Days, and Summer Academies

- **AIW lead and local coach development** to build capacity in additional schools

Actual financial support for AIW PD has varied considerably. From a sample of high schools with 10 teachers on pilot teams, costs in year 1 ranged from $1,440 to $3,550 per teacher involved in AIW teams. Consistently, however, the average costs devoted to AIW PD at a school decreased after the first year of implementation, from about $19,000 in year 1 to $10,000 in years 2 and 3. In Iowa, financial support from the Department of Education helped some schools considerably, especially in the first 2 to 3 years of implementation. Figure 7.5 shows how the Department of Education and local schools or districts shared costs and how the percentage of average state costs declined from year 1 to year 3 of implementation. As more teachers became involved, school and agency leaders instituted structures and practices for PD that, often through reallocation of staff assignments, had low or no costs, such as common planning periods and late start or early release days.

The Iowa Department of Education increased its percentage of funding in year 2 because the number of teachers participating in AIW PD doubled and sometimes tripled as a school moved from one or two pilot teams to many teams. However, after 3 or 4 years, when most schools shifted to AIW PD as their primary focus with all teachers participating, the school could reallocate its own resources to support the work. Schools beyond year 3 no longer received state funds, and schools in year 3 and beyond took on more of the costs through local school or district funds.

**Figure 7.5  Percentage of AIW Costs From Department of Education (DE) and Schools/ Districts (LEA)**

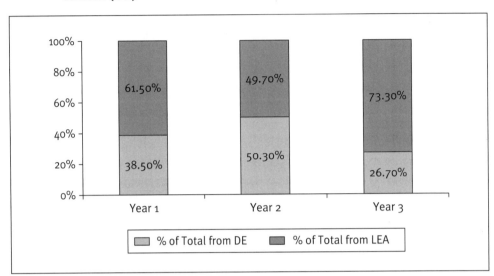

## SUMMARY AND CONCLUSION

Notorious failures in the history of instructional reform can be explained by three common errors of policymakers and administrators. First, policymakers and external agencies continually introduce too many new initiatives that are often contradictory or not well supported by research. Second, when approaches have been well researched, they are abandoned before enough capacity for implementation is built to give them a fair trial, thereby compromising initially promising results. Lastly, in the zeal to go to scale, promising research-based reforms are prematurely ramped up before initial adopters have built the capacity to sustain them.

In contrast, AIW professional development helps to minimize these tendencies by insisting on an intellectual focus for teaching that can integrate and even help to reduce other distracting reforms. For example, as science teachers learn to implement rigorous scientific inquiry lessons and tasks with their students, language arts teachers can complement this with assignments for elaborated writing to present strong arguments grounded in textual evidence. AIW professional development, supported with external lead coaches, reinforces similar coordination across all disciplines and grade levels. As Laura Hensley, from the West Sioux District in Iowa, explained,

> When I sit with my AIW colleagues and score a task, student work, or instruction, I'm empowered by teachers leading teachers. Together we break down the barriers of isolation and help each other become better professionals in the classroom by creating student work that is meaningful and purposeful. I hear

feedback that is productive and constructive without being critical or evaluative of my personal attributes.

Similarly, partnerships and networking among schools on AIW instruction can break down barriers of isolation, strengthening a system's program coherence and capacity to deepen and sustain learning for more schools in a district, region, or state.

This chapter compliments the school-level focus of Chapter 6 by describing important extensions of AIW professional development beyond the first few years in one school. We have explained how leaders in external agencies can help to expand and deepen implementation in an initial school; enhance the knowledge and skills of teacher leaders as they transition to become AIW local coaches; develop structures and resources that sustain implementation with new teachers or administrators; and address incoherence when other initiatives in curriculum, testing, or professional development diminish attention to teaching for AIW.

The way different agencies relate to one another and the order in which they become involved will vary according to specific professional needs in different contexts. Like good instruction for students, professional development for teachers and administrators must be differentiated but always focused on the learning targets of the AIW framework. The history of our AIW work with external agencies shows how, at different times, actors in district offices and in regional and state agencies offered critical support, guided by collaboration with the Center.

Authentic Intellectual Work is a compelling framework for addressing the current calls for more engaging, meaningful, and rigorous learning opportunities for diverse learners. AIW supports implementation of the Common Core State Standards as well as other challenging content standards in different subject areas. A body of research that extends over 20 years, and includes a range of schools and students across the United States, consistently shows the power of AIW for both improved and more equitable student outcomes.

The distinctive criteria for Authentic Intellectual Work are *construction of knowledge* through the use of *disciplined inquiry* to produce discourse, products, or performances that have *value beyond school*. The AIW framework sets standards for teaching that

- maximizes expectations of intellectual rigor for all students,

- increases student interest in academic work,

- supports teachers to take time to teach for in-depth understanding,

- provides a common conception of student intellectual work that promotes professional community among teachers of different grade levels and subjects, and

- equips students to address the complex intellectual challenges of work, civic participation, and managing personal affairs in the contemporary world.

We have described the framework and its rationale; illustrated each of the three criteria with examples of instruction and student work along with standards and rubrics that further define the criteria; summarized the related body of research; and described what we've learned about AIW implementation over 8 years of professional development with teachers, administrators, and district and state leaders.

AIW professional development offers no easy or quick formula for transforming instruction to support rigorous intellectual work; there aren't any. Approaches that dominate schooling with lower order thinking and superficial treatment of too much content that lacks connection to students and to real-world problems have persistently resisted change. But our experience with AIW professional development shows that instruction can be transformed. Leaders at one school put it this way: "AIW is an education change maker. Unlike other initiatives, the organic nature of AIW takes teachers where they are in their own work and provides a framework for all teachers to improve their instructional practices" (Briese, Dirkx, Mueting, & Wiemers, in press). Teachers and administrators in numerous schools and districts now engage in the complex intellectual work and collaborative inquiry on the standards for intellectual rigor in students' schoolwork that the AIW process requires. We hope this book inspires more educators to embark with students on a journey toward more Authentic Intellectual Work.

# Appendix

## ELABORATION OF AIW RESEARCH

Figures A.1 and A.2 summarize the main studies. These studies compared the performance of students taught by teachers who received higher scores on promotion of Authentic Intellectual Work according to our criteria for instruction and teachers' assignments (e.g., teachers who scored in the highest quartile of the group of teachers studied) with the performance of students whose teachers received lower scores on promotion of Authentic Intellectual Work (e.g., teachers who scored in the lowest quartile of the group of teachers studied).

**Figure A.1  Research Measuring Student Achievement With Standards for Authentic Intellectual Work**

| Study | Number and Type of Schools, Classes, and Students | Subjects and Grade Levels | Instruction Observed or Surveyed | Assignments Collected | Achievement Measure | Achievement Benefit of Higher vs. Lower Scoring Teachers' Classes |
|---|---|---|---|---|---|---|
| Center on Organization and Restructuring of Schools (CORS) Field Study, 1990–1994 (Newmann, Marks, & Gamoran, 1996) | • 24 elementary, middle, and high schools<br>• 130 classrooms<br>• 2,100 students<br>• Mostly urban, some non-urban schools | • Math, social studies<br>• Grades 4–5, 7–8, 9–10 | Observed | Yes | AIW rubrics | 30 percentile points higher than lower scoring |
| Chicago Annenberg Research Project Field Study, 1996–1997 (Newmann, Lopez, & Bryk, 1998) | • 12 Chicago elementary schools<br>• 74 teachers<br>• About 700 students, all urban | • Language arts (writing), math<br>• Grades 3, 6, 8 | No | Yes | AIW rubrics | 34–56 percentile points higher than lower scoring |
| Minnesota Observed Instruction Study, 1998 (Avery, 1999) | • 1 urban high school<br>• 5 teachers<br>• 12 classes<br>• 116 students | • Social studies<br>• Grade 11 | Observed | No; all classes had same high-scoring authentic assignment. | AIW rubrics | 66% higher scores on rubric than lower scoring |

*(Continued)*

**(Continued)**

| Study | Number and Type of Schools, Classes, and Students | Subjects and Grade Levels | Instruction Observed or Surveyed | Assignments Collected | Achievement Measure | Achievement Benefit of Higher vs. Lower Scoring Teachers' Classes |
|---|---|---|---|---|---|---|
| Research Institute on Secondary Education Reform for Youth With Disabilities (RISER) Study, 1999–2003 (King, Schroeder, & Chawszczewski, 2006) | • 4 high schools<br>• 32 teachers<br>• 32 classes<br>• 650 students<br>• Urban, rural, and small city schools | • English, math, social studies, science<br>• Grades 9–12 | Observed | Yes | AIW rubrics | 51%–58% higher scores on rubric than lower scoring |
| Systemic Implications of Pedagogy and Achievement in NSW Public Schools study (SIPA), 2002–2007 (Ladwig, Smith, Gore, Amosa, & Griffiths, 2007) | • 26 schools (15 primary, 11 secondary)<br>• 2,236 students (640 primary, 734 secondary)<br>• Urban and rural schools with students of high, medium, and low socioeconomic status | • Math, science, English, human society and Its environment, personal development, health and physical education<br>• Years 4, 6 8 | No | Yes | AIW rubrics | 15 percentile points higher than lower scoring (estimated)* |

Study did not report benefits of high-vs. lower-scoring classes on authentic pedagogy. Benefits are estimated here by hypothetically comparing students scoring one standard deviation below and one standard deviation above the mean using the study's reported effect size of 0.21 (Ladwig et al., 2007, Table 3) and estimating the percentile advantage (Johns Hopkins University, n.d.) showing effect sizes associated with percentile gains in normal distributions.

Chapter 5 described two studies in more detail, one that measured achievement according to criteria for Authentic Intellectual Work and one that measured achievement with standardized tests. We describe two additional studies below.

### The Chicago 12-School Study (K–8)—Authentic Student Achievement

In the spring semester of 1997, 74 teachers of language arts and mathematics in Grades 3, 6, and 8 in 12 Chicago elementary schools that scored below the average of all Chicago elementary schools submitted four student assignments, two of which they considered to pose challenging assessments of the students' understanding of the subject. Teachers also submitted students' written work in response to the assignments. Chicago language arts and mathematics teachers at the same grade levels not participating in the study scored the quality of demands for Authentic Intellectual Work in the assignments and the quality of authentic achievement evident in students' responses.

**Figure A.2  Research Measuring Student Achievement With Conventional Standardized Tests**

| Study | Number and Type of Schools, Classes, and Students | Subjects and Grade Levels | Instruction Observed or Surveyed | Assignments Collected | Achievement Measure | Achievement Difference Between Higher and Lower Scoring Teachers' Classes |
|---|---|---|---|---|---|---|
| National Education Longitudinal Study (NELS), 1988–1992 (Lee & Smith, 1996; Lee, Smith, & Croninger, 1997) | • 1,000 high schools, national representative sample<br>• 10,000 students | • Math, science<br>• Grades 8, 10, 12 | Surveyed | No | NAEP, multiple choice | Grade 8–10 gain 60%–80% higher; Grade 10–12 gain 100% higher on test score scale |
| Chicago Annenberg Research Project. Authentic Assignments and Standardized Test (ITBS) Gains, 1997–1999 (Newmann, Bryk, & Nagaoka, 2001) | • 46 Chicago elementary schools<br>• 124 teachers<br>• About 1,600 students per grade per subject | • Math, writing, reading | No | Yes | Iowa Tests of Basic Skills | Yearly gains 40% higher on test score scale |
| Authentic Pedagogy in Social Studies Classrooms and Relationship to Student Performance on State-Mandated Tests, 2008–2011 (Saye & Social Studies Inquiry Research Collaborative, 2013) | • 6 states<br>• 17 schools<br>• 52 teachers<br>• 93 classes<br>• 2,020 students | • Social studies<br>• Grades 8–11 | Yes | Yes | State-mandated tests | 22 percentile point advantage* |

Study did not report percentile benefits of high-vs. lower-scoring classes on authentic pedagogy. Benefits are estimated here by hypothetically comparing students scoring one standard deviation below and one standard deviation above the mean using the study's reported effect size of 0.276 (Saye et al., 2013, Table 5) and estimating the percentile advantage (Johns Hopkins University, n.d.) showing effect sizes associated with percentile gains in normal distributions.

Figure A.3 compares the percentile ranking of average student scores with teachers whose assignments scored in the lowest versus highest quartiles among all the classes. Students receiving the highest quality assignments scored from 30 to 56 percentiles higher than students of teachers who gave the lowest quality assignments.

These and the other studies included in Figure A.1 have shown consistent benefits for students in authentic intellectual performance across grade levels and subjects of teachers making demands for Authentic Intellectual Work.

## The NELS 1,000-High School Study—Conventional Student Achievement

From 1988 to 1992 the National Educational Longitudinal Study (NELS) included surveys and testing that followed 10,000 students in 1,000 U.S. schools in Grades 8–12. Some items in the teacher and student surveys of instruction in

**Figure A.3  Writing and Mathematics Student Performance According to Authentic Intellectual Quality of Teachers' Assignments**

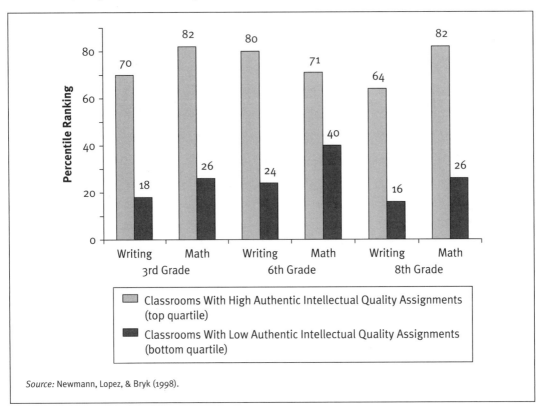

*Source:* Newmann, Lopez, & Bryk (1998).

mathematics and science were consistent with our standards for authentic instruction. We used these items to estimate the degree of authentic intellectual demands that students experienced. All students were tested in these and other subjects using items, usually multiple choice, from the National Assessment of Student Progress (NAEP). Most of these items required only recall or simple application of previously learned information, rather than construction of knowledge, in-depth understanding, or elaborated communication. Figure A.4 shows the differences in test score gains from Grades 8–10 and Grades 10–12 between students receiving below-average versus above-average levels of authentic instruction.

Gains in achievement are reported here as standardized scores of gains in items answered correctly, on scales that adjust the percentage of correct items according to the difficulty of the items. While the scales are not easily interpreted in terms of percentile gains or other common measures, the advantage of high- versus low-quality instruction is substantial in both subjects and both 2-year comparison periods.

**Figure A.4  High School Mathematics and Science, Conventional Achievement Gains According to Levels of Authentic Instruction**

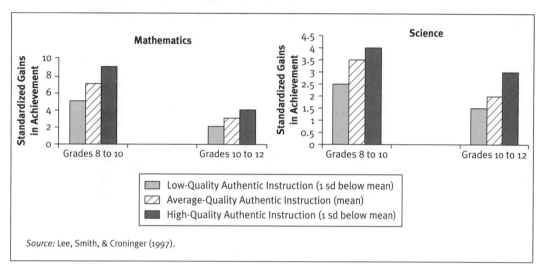

*Source:* Lee, Smith, & Croninger (1997).

In a recent study by Kim et al. (2012), approximately 3,300 K–3 students from six Title I schools were assigned to experimental or control classes (total classes = 115) on a random basis. Experimental students were exposed to a concept-based science curriculum that emphasized deep learning through concept mastery and investigation, whereas control classes learned science from traditional school-based curricula. AIW rubrics were not used, but the curriculum's emphasis on deep learning is consistent with the AIW emphasis on higher order thinking and deep knowledge. After controlling for student prior achievement, and using a standardized measure of student achievement in science (the MAT-8 science subtest) and a standardized measure of critical thinking, all ability groups of students benefited from an inquiry-based approach to learning that emphasized science concepts, and there was a positive achievement effect for young children of low socioeconomic status who were exposed to such a curriculum. Complexities in the design of the study make it difficult to estimate an overall effect size attributable to the experimental curriculum, but in several comparisons, significant differences in achievement favored the experimental group over the control group (Kim et al., 2012).

The discussion of equity in Chapter 5 mentioned positive findings from the RISER study (see Figure A.1), whose results are illustrated in Figure A.5.

**Figure A.5  Authentic Performance for Students With and Without Disabilities in Classes With Low- and High-Scoring Authentic Assignments**

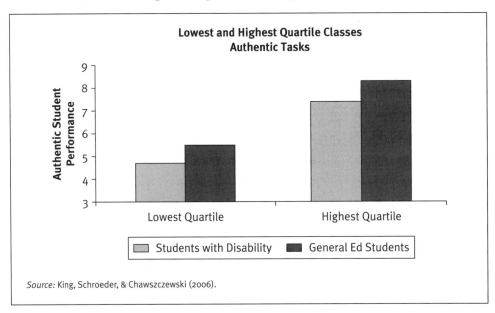

*Source:* King, Schroeder, & Chawszczewski (2006).

Figures A.6a and A.6b show the effects of authentic instruction on equity as it relates to students' socioeconomic status. While authentic pedagogy does not eliminate gaps, it often helps reduce educational inequality in student achievement. (Figures A.6a and A.6b were created from Lee & Smith, 1995; Lee, Smith, & Croninger, 1995, 1997.)

**Figure A.6a  Effects of Low Authentic Instruction on Science Achievement Gaps Between Students of Low and High Socioeconomic Status**

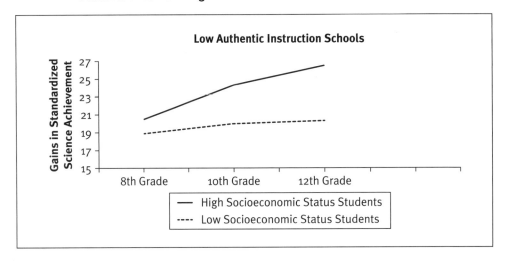

**Figure A.6b  Effects of High Authentic Instruction on Science Achievement Gaps Between Students of Low and High Socioeconomic Status**

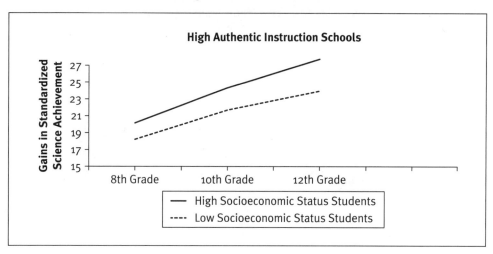

Chapter 5 also summarized an evaluation of AIW professional development on student achievement, as measured by standardized tests in Iowa, either the Iowa Test of Basic Skills (ITBS) or the Iowa Test of Educational Development (ITED). Students in AIW schools generally scored higher than students in a matched control group of schools without AIW professional development. Details are shown in Figures A.7, A.8, A.9, and A.10. Differences between the two groups of students that are not statistically significant (and therefore assumed to be due to chance, rather than differences in instructional programming) are marked with an asterisk (*).

**Figure A.7  ITBS/ITED Results in Reading**

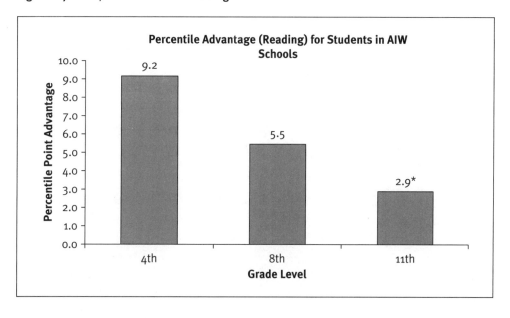

**Figure A.8  ITBS/ITED Results in Math**

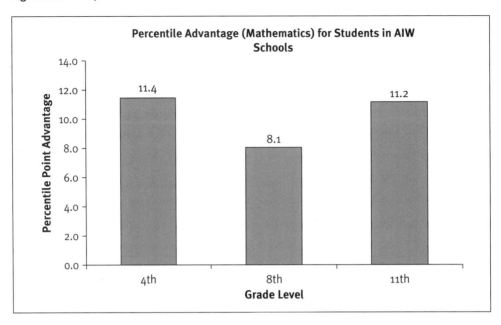

**Figure A.9  ITBS/ITED Results in Science**

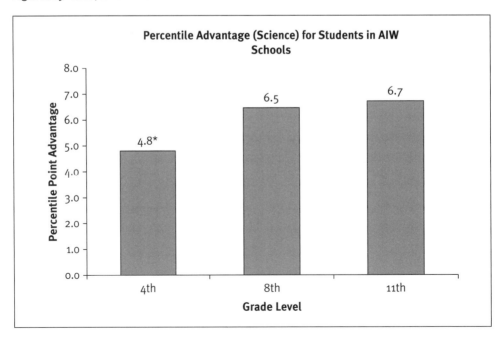

**Figure A.10   ITBS/ITED Results in Social Studies**

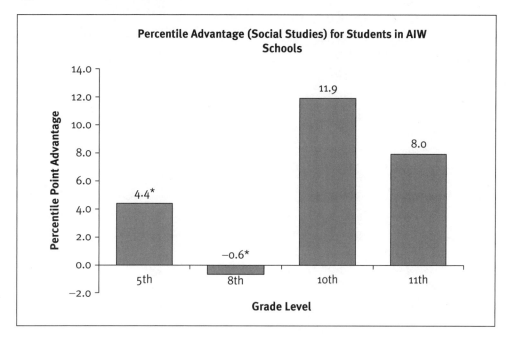

*Note:* Because of the considerably lower number of tested students in social studies, we analyzed only grade levels with more than 100 students with social studies data in the AIW schools and the non-AIW schools. As a result, Grades 5 (rather than 4), 8, and 11 are reported for social studies.

# References

Aristotle. (1946). *The politics of Aristotle* (Ernest Barker, Trans.). Oxford, UK: Clarendon Press.

Avery, P. G. (1999). Authentic instruction and assessment. *Social Education, 65,* 368–373.

Avery, P. G., Freeman, C., & Carmichael-Tanaka, D. L. (2002). Developing authentic instruction in the social studies. *Journal of Research in Education, 12*(1), 50–56.

Barber, B. R. (1984). *Strong democracy: Participatory politics for a new age.* Berkeley: University of California Press.

Bransford, J. D., Brown, A. L., & Cocking, R. R. (2000). *How people learn: Brain, mind, experience, and school.* Washington, DC: National Academy Press.

Bridgeland, J. M., DiIulio, J. J., Jr., & Morison, K. B. (2006). *The silent epidemic: Perspectives of high school dropouts.* Washington, DC: Civic Enterprises.

Briese, P., Dirkx, M., Mueting, J., & Wiemers, E. (in press). Infusing authentic intellectual work into the curriculum. In M. B. King (Ed.), *Schools and districts meeting rigorous standards through authentic intellectual work.* Thousand Oaks, CA: Corwin.

Cappelli, P., Bassi, L., Katz, D., Knoke, D., Osterman, P., & Useem, M. (1997). *Change at work.* New York, NY: Oxford University Press.

Carmichael, D. L., & Martens R. P. (in press). Professional learning for authentic intellectual work: Iowa's statewide initiative. In M. B. King (Ed.), *Schools and districts meeting rigorous standards through authentic intellectual work.* Thousand Oaks, CA: Corwin.

Carmichael, D., Martens, R. P., Zirps, J. B., Wahlert, C., & Peterson, S. (2013). *The AIW journey: A guide for reflective practice.* Minneapolis, MN: Itasca Press.

Carmichael, D. L., & Wahlert, C. M. (2014). *The coaching companion: Transforming teaching and learning through authentic intellectual work* (2nd ed.). Saint Paul, MN: Center for AIW.

Case, R. (2013). The unfortunate consequences of Bloom's taxonomy. *Social Education, 77,* 196–200.

Childress, S., Elmore, R. F., Grossman, A. S., & Johnson, S. M. (Eds.). (2007). *Managing school districts for high performance: Cases in public education leadership*. Cambridge, MA: Harvard Education Press.

Christakos, N. A., & Fowler, J. H. (2009). *Connected: The surprising power of our social networks and how they shape our lives*. New York, NY: Little, Brown.

Cuban, L. (2013). *Inside the black box of classroom practice: Change without reform in American education*. Cambridge, MA: Harvard Education Press.

Decker, P. T., Rice, J. K., Moore, M. T., & Rollefson, M. R. (1997). *Education and the economy: An indicators report*. Washington, DC: U.S. Department of Education, Office of Educational Research and Improvement, National Center for Education Statistics.

Dewey, J. (1966). *Democracy and education*. New York, NY: Free Press. (Original work published 1916).

Dweck, C. (2006). *Mindset: The new psychology of success*. New York, NY: Ballentine Books.

Elmore, R. (2000). *Building a new structure for school leadership*. Washington, DC: Albert Shanker Institute.

Elmore, R. (2002). *Bridging the gap between standards and achievement: The imperative for professional development in education*. Washington, DC: Albert Shanker Institute.

Erickson, L. H. (2002). *Concept-based curriculum and instruction: Teaching beyond the facts*. Thousand Oaks, CA: Corwin.

Fullan, M. (2001). *Leading in a culture of change*. San Francisco, CA: Jossey-Bass.

Honig, M. I. (2008). District central offices as learning organizations: How sociocultural and organizational learning theories elaborate district central office administrators' participation in teaching and learning improvement efforts. *American Journal of Education, 114*, 627–664.

Iowa Department of Education. (2012a). Addendum to *An initial evaluation of the Iowa DE project to enhance authentic intellectual work Fall 2007 to Fall 2011*. Des Moines: Author. Retrieved from https://www.educateiowa.gov/sites/files/ed/documents/AddendumToMay2012AIWReport2013-03-08.pdf

Iowa Department of Education. (2012b). *An initial evaluation of the Iowa DE project to enhance authentic intellectual work Fall 2007 to Fall 2011*. Des Moines: Author. Retrieved from https://www.educateiowa.gov/sites/files/ed/documents/AIWEvaluationReportFinal.pdf

Jefferson, T. (1939). *Democracy* (S. K. Padover, Ed.). New York, NY: D. Appleton-Century.

Johns Hopkins University. (n.d.). *Review methods: Interpreting effects sizes.* Retrieved from http://www.bestevidence.org/methods/effectsize.htm

Jussim, L., & Harber, K. D. (2005). Teacher expectations and self-fulfilling prophecies: Knowns and unknowns, resolved and unresolved controversies. *Personality and Social Psychology Review, 9*(2), 131–155.

Kane, M. B., Khattri, N., Reeve, A. L., Adamson, R. J., & Pelavin Research Institute. (1995). *Assessment of student performance: Studies of education reform* (3 vols.). Washington, DC: U.S. Department of Education, Office of Educational Research and Improvement.

Kim, K. H., VanTassel-Baska, J., Bracken, B. A., Feng, A., Stambaugh, T. & Bland, L. (2012). Project Clarion: Three years of science instruction in Title I schools among K–third grade students. *Research in Science Education, 42*, 813–829.

King, M. B. (Ed.). (in press). *Schools and districts meeting rigorous standards through authentic intellectual work.* Thousand Oaks, CA: Corwin.

King, M. B., & Bouchard, K. (2011). The capacity to build organizational capacity in schools. *Journal of Educational Administration, 49(6),* 653–669.

King, M. B., Schroeder, J. L., & Chawszczewski, D. (2006). Authentic assessment and student performance in inclusive secondary schools. In F. W. Parkay, E. J. Anctil, & G. J. Hass (Eds.), *Curriculum planning: A contemporary approach* (8th ed., pp. 199–207). Boston, MA: Allyn & Bacon.

Ladwig, J., Smith, M., Gore, J., Amosa, W., & Griffiths, T. (2007). *Quality of pedagogy and student achievement: Multi-level replication of authentic pedagogy.* Paper presented at the Australian Association for Research in Education conference, Fremantle, Western Australia.

Lee, V. E., & Smith, J. B. (1995). Effects of high school restructuring and size on early gains in achievement and engagement. *Sociology of Education, 68*, 241–270.

Lee, V. E., & Smith, J. (1996). Collective responsibility for learning and its effects on gains in achievement and engagement for early secondary school students. *American Journal of Education, 104*, 103–147.

Lee, V. E., Smith, J., & Croninger, R. (1995). Another look at high school restructuring. *Issues in Restructuring Schools, 9.* Madison, WI: Center on Organization and Restructuring of Schools, Wisconsin Center for Education Research, University of Wisconsin. Retrieved from http://www.wcer.wisc.edu/archive/cors/Issues_in_Restructuring_Schools

Lee, V. E., Smith, J., & Croninger, R. (1997). How high school organization influences the equitable distribution of learning in mathematics and science. *Sociology of Education, 70,* 128–150.

Lieberman, A., & Miller, L. (2007). Transforming professional development: Understanding and organizing learning communities. In W. D. Hawley (Ed.), *The keys to effective schools* (pp. 99–116). Thousand Oaks, CA: Corwin.

Louis, K. S., Kruse, S. D., & Marks, H. M. (1996). Schoolwide professional community. In F. M. Newmann & Associates, *Authentic achievement: Restructuring schools for intellectual quality* (pp. 179–203). San Francisco, CA: Jossey-Bass.

Marks, H. M. (2000). Student engagement in instructional activity: Patterns in elementary, middle and high schools. *American Educational Research Journal, 37,* 153–184.

Murnane, R. J., & Levy, F. (1996). *Teaching the new basic skills: Principles for children to thrive in a changing economy.* New York, NY: Free Press.

National Center on Education and the Economy. (1990). *America's choice: High skills or low wages? The report of the Commission on the Skills of the American Workforce.* Rochester, NY: Author.

Newmann, F. M., & Associates. (1996). *Authentic achievement: Restructuring schools for intellectual quality.* San Francisco, CA: Jossey-Bass.

Newmann, F. M., Bryk, A. S., & Nagaoka, J. (2001). *Authentic intellectual work and standardized tests: Conflict or coexistence.* Chicago, IL: Consortium on Chicago School Research.

Newmann, F. M., King, M. B., & Carmichael, D. L. (2007). *Authentic instruction and assessment: Common standards for rigor and relevance in teaching academic subjects.* Des Moines: Iowa Department of Education.

Newmann, F. M., King, M. B., & Carmichael, D. L. (2009). *Teaching for authentic intellectual work: Standards and scoring criteria for teachers' tasks, student performance, and instruction.* Minneapolis, MN: Tasora Books.

Newmann, F. M., Lopez, G., & Bryk, A. S. (1998). *The quality of intellectual work in Chicago schools: A baseline report.* Chicago, IL: Consortium on Chicago School Research.

Newmann, F. M., Marks, H. M., & Gamoran, A. (1996). Authentic pedagogy and student performance. *American Journal of Education, 104,* 280–312.

Newmann, F. M., Secada, W. G., & Wehlage, G. G. (1995). *A guide to authentic instruction and assessment: Vision, standards, and scoring.* Madison: University of Wisconsin, Wisconsin Center for Education Research.

Newmann, F. M., Smith, B. A, Allensworth, E., & Bryk, A. S. (2001). Instructional program coherence: What it is and why it should guide school improvement policy. *Educational Evaluation and Policy Analysis, 23*, 297–321.

Payne, C. M. (2008). *So much reform, so little change: The persistence of failure in urban schools.* Cambridge, MA: Harvard Education Press.

Saye, J., & Social Studies Inquiry Research Collaborative. (2013). Authentic pedagogy: Its presence in social studies classrooms and relationship to student performance on state-mandated tests. *Theory and Research in Social Education, 41*(1), 89–132.

Slavin, R. E. (1998). Sand, bricks, and seeds: School change strategies and readiness for reform. In A. Hargreaves, A. Lieberman, M. Fullan, & D. Hopkins (Eds.), *International handbook of educational change* (pp. 1299–1313). Boston, MA: Kluwer Academic.

Weick, K. E. (1976). Educational organizations as loosely coupled systems. *Administrative Science Quarterly, 21,* 1–19.

# Notes

## CHAPTER 1

1. Part II of this book offers more examples of how teachers' instruction and assignments can demand, and student work can demonstrate, high levels of Authentic Intellectual Work.

2. Louis, Kruse, and Marks (1996) showed that schools with higher levels of professional community were more likely to show higher levels of authentic pedagogy.

3. Chapter 5 and the Appendix give details on the research.

## CHAPTER 2

1. All rubrics and standards included in Chapters 2, 3, and 4 are from Newmann, King, and Carmichael (2009). While we include the entire rubric for some examples, others have only the criterion for the highest score.

2. The goal for this lesson is for students to apply the addition strategies they have learned to a real-world situation with which they are familiar.

3. Students were given the assignment only in Spanish.

4. The scoring rubric here, for a non-core subject assignment, is basically the same as the one shown for mathematics. We simply substitute thinking about content in another subject, in this case Spanish, for mathematical thinking.

## CHAPTER 4

1. For an overview of this project, watch the video "AIW Transformation— Monticello CSD" at www.youtube.com/watch?v=48-Lg_yibBM&feature=youtube.

## CHAPTER 5

1. The studies were based at the Wisconsin Center for Education Research at the University of Wisconsin-Madison (Center on Organization and Restructuring of Schools and Research Institute on Secondary Reform for Youth with Disabilities), the University of Minnesota, and the Consortium on Chicago School Research.

2. Other design details are in the Appendix, Figure A.1.

3. In some schools there were two teachers per grade, one for math and one for language arts, but in other schools one teacher in a grade taught both subjects.

4. Other design details are in the Appendix, Figure A.2.

5. For a comprehensive summary of research in this field, see Jussim & Harber (2005).

6. Gains derived from data presented in Lee and Smith (1996); Lee, Smith, and Croninger (1997).

7. For example, in the original national study of 24 schools, if the scores for instruction were scaled from 1 to 100, the highest scoring teacher would have received a score of 67 and the average score for instruction among all teachers would have been only 33 (see Newmann & Associates, 1996).

8. The evaluation report, published first in 2012 consists of two parts. See Iowa Department of Education (2012a, 2012b).

9. A study with this design is now under way. See *An Evaluation of the Authentic Intellectual Work Initiative in Iowa,* http://wceruw.org/projects/projects. php?project_num=1068.

10. Details are given in the Appendix, Figures A.7–A.10.

11. Effect size is a measure of the strength of an initiative or intervention by comparing differences between groups. In this study, across all subjects and grades we found an average effect size of .46. This means that an average-scoring student in an AIW school would score about 30 percentile points higher than an average-scoring student in a matched control school. In most educational interventions an effect size of .30 or above is considered important. See www.uccs.edu/lbecker/ effect-size.html.

# Index

A SAGE Company

Helping educators make the greatest impact

**CORWIN HAS ONE MISSION:** to enhance education through intentional professional learning.

We build long-term relationships with our authors, educators, clients, and associations who partner with us to develop and continuously improve the best evidence-based practices that establish and support lifelong learning.

# Solutions you want. Experts you trust. Results you need.